PRAISE FC ...—. — ιντλι N

Jill Celeste doesn't shy away from the hard discussions that need to be had in today's world. From sexism, racism, and white privilege to bullying, boundaries, and support, *Loud Woman* explores the nuances of how women were taught to behave and how it works against us in the quest for equality and understanding. Peppered with lessons from her own life, Jill brilliantly illustrates what it takes to become a Loud Woman and the advantages of doing so. You can't read this book without be moved to step up your game, stand in your truth, and tell your inner good girl to hush!

— CHERI D. ANDREWS, ESQ., SMALL BUSINESS
ATTORNEY, AND AUTHOR OF *SMOOTH SAILING:*
A PRACTICAL GUIDE TO
LEGALLY PROTECTING YOUR BUSINESS

Being a Loud Woman has little to do with volume and everything to do with owning our worth and boldly speaking our truth. In *Loud Woman*, Jill Celeste beautifully illustrates, often through personal stories, the many ways we remain 'quiet,' what it costs us, and how everyone loses when we hide our gifts and talents, and remain small. If you are ready to break free and claim your rightful space in the world, this book is for you!

— NICOLETTE BLANCO, AUTHOR OF *BY A THREAD,*
RESILIENCE STRATEGIES FOR THE
PARTIALLY UNRAVELED

Loud Woman is a raw, emotional and honest look at Jill's journey. Using her techniques and strategies, you'll learn to cope with your own challenges to reach your own personal goals. It is time to stand up, speak up, and use your own voice to change your world.

— KAREN CAMPBELL, ENTREPRENEUR, CAMPBELL'S SCOTTISH TERRIERS

Jill shares her story to help us become what she knows we are meant to be. I found myself nodding along; what she's writing about herself could easily been about me. I picked up *Loud Woman* at a time of chaos in my life, wondering what my greater purpose would be. I was on a journey to find my next step. When I had finally determined what I wanted to do, *Loud Woman* was that voice in my ear to push me to do it. I am so grateful Jill shared this voice with me. You will not be disappointed when you open your heart to the impact of her message.

— ELIZABETH CERANOWSKI, SENIOR MANAGER, SOFTWARE–MARKETING EDUCATION, LENOVO

Loud Woman was uniquely useful in asking me to consider how well I support or disempower other women. It was definitely a wake-up call to be intentional about supporting other women. She explained how we can even support women whose political views are not aligned with ours. And Jill had the courage to speak to privileged white women like me about the insidious power of racism, and how to not support or encourage that wicked belief system. This is a book I will look to when I am stuck figuring out how to navigate a situation that calls for Loud Woman Courage. You might find me thinking, 'What would Jill do?'

— MARIBETH COYE DECKER, INTUITIVE ANIMAL COMMUNICATOR AND HEALER, AUTHOR OF *PEACE IN PASSING: COMFORT FOR LOVING HUMANS DURING ANIMAL TRANSITIONS*

Many women live in regular fear of not being good enough... *Am I too much? Am I not enough? Will they like me if I'm the real me?* That's when they overcompensate by being 'the nice girl' and become addicted to people pleasing, to their own detriment. It doesn't have to be this way. You can absolutely create a life you love, without resentment, without wondering if this is all there is to life. No more Quiet Mouse. It's time we hear you roar as the fullest expression of who you were made to be. Here's to your beautiful transformation.

— FABIENNE FREDRICKSON, FOUNDER OF FABIENNE.COM AND AUTHOR OF *EMBRACE YOUR MAGNIFICENCE: GET OUT OF YOUR OWN WAY AND LIVE A RICHER, FULLER, MORE ABUNDANT LIFE*

Sometimes we need a permission slip: A little reminder of who we are and what we came into this life to do. Jill Celeste's *Loud Woman* is that reminder. A story lovingly told with a bold voice, unceasing wit, and a willingness to 'go there,' I recommend this book when you are looking to reclaim your place and remember exactly who you are.

— BAILEY FRUMAN, MSW, LCSW, PSYCHOTHERAPIST, SPEAKER, FOUNDER OF MINDRISE, AND AUTHOR, *OWN YOUR POWER: YOUR GUIDE TO BEING POWERFUL, FEARLESS, AND FREE*

Loud Woman feels like an intimate conversation with a long-lost girlfriend where she tells you stories over coffee, painting a picture of a woman learning how to be her own best champion while also lifting up the women around her. In it, Jill lends smart, actionable advice on setting boundaries and creating space for yourself in your life, honoring your relationships, and stepping out of your comfort zone. *Loud Woman* reminds us to get out of our own way, and to not be afraid of the loudest voice in your head: your own.

— PATTY GAFFNEY, MANAGER, STAGING OPERATIONS, NBC

Loud Woman reveals and explores those stifling moments every "quiet women" experiences when taking on roles of leadership or even speaking for herself for the first time in this 'man's world.' After applying these simple tools, you will no longer find yourself going over what happened in your mind with that tell-tale 'I should have said this instead.' We all need training wheels after this long period of time away from our work groups and people. *Loud Woman* will help you speak up effectively and productively.

— JOAN HEPSWORTH, BOOKSELLER AND OWNER, THE
PAPERBACK EXCHANGE BOOKSTORE

Even as a well-versed women's and gender studies professor, *Loud Woman* gave me concrete ways that I could own my empowerment *right here, right now*. Within a day of starting the book, I walked taller and spoke more directly, and my marriage and health have already improved significantly simply because of the lessons contained in this book.

— KARI NIXON, ASSISTANT PROFESSOR, WHITWORTH
UNIVERSITY, AND AUTHOR, *QUARANTINE LIFE FROM
CHOLERA TO COVID-19*

Loud Woman is for all the women out there whose actions and words are framed by what others have defined as 'acceptable.' Drawing from reflections on her own life experiences and observations about those of others, Jill Celeste shares how societal expectations keep many women small and quiet, and she explains what they can do to find their voice. It is her mission to encourage and support women to speak up for themselves and each other. This book is a thought-provoking call to action.

— JUDY KANE, AUTHOR OF *YOUR 4TRUTHS*

LOUD WOMAN

INTRODUCTION

Often times, the most righteous thing you can do is shake the
table.

— ALEXANDRIA OCASIO-CORTEZ

BIASES

I am white...

This book is told from the perspective of a white American woman — with all the unintentional biases therein. I have done my best to address my areas of white privilege but know my journey is far from perfect. Thank you in advance for your patience for any prejudices in this book, and please accept my apologies if I have offended or hurt you in any way. I am learning to do better, I promise.

I am a woman...

I identify as a woman. I respect all gender identifications. In this book, I will use terms such as girl, boy, he, she, woman, and man, but please know I believe gender is how *you* define it. I hope you will find the overarching themes and lessons to be inclusive, no matter how you identify.

I am liberal...

I could not write a memoir/self-help book without weaving in my liberal ideology. With that said, Conservative Loud Women, this book will still help you. We need you to be Loud, too.

A LOUD WOMAN

W hose budget will be paying for this?" I asked, as I scribbled down the instructions from the vice president and directors sitting around the conference room table. We were meeting about a new patient safety initiative, and the management team had a laundry list of items they needed my marketing team to create.

"Don't worry about that," the vice president responded, irritation edging her voice.

I did have to worry about it though. As a marketing manager, knowing who was paying for a project was an important part of my job.

I eyed the vice president, willing her to answer me. She flipped the page over in her notebook and scratched down something on the page. I never did get an answer to my budget question.

The next day, my director pulled me into her office. She had just met with this same vice president, who told my director that I was "out of line" for asking the budget question and my tone was "disrespectful." The vice president then told my director that I was not there to ask questions. I was there to gather information so I could "do my job."

I almost laughed. I should have guessed that my question would not be appreciated; it was so typical of the political bullshit that permeated from my employer.

Despite my inclination to laugh, I also was bewildered: *How am I supposed to do my job if I can't ask questions?*

Here's the thing: I was getting counseled for asking a budget question; however, I knew it was much more than that.

What I was *really* being counseled on was my Loudness—how I spoke up, how I asked for what I wanted, how I had boundaries around my time, and how I did not tolerate being interrupted.

What I *really* was being asked to do was to take up less space, keep my mouth shut, and do my job in the quietest way possible.

My employer embodied a classic patriarchal structure. Most of our senior management team were older white guys. Our outdated dress code specified skirt lengths, panty hose requirements, and no open toe shoes (even during Florida summers).

On the surface, my employer looked like a great place for women to work, and it was, as long as women played by the rules, which included deferring to men in positions above us and not rocking the boat (or in my case, asking questions about the marketing budget).

In other words, we were expected to Quiet.

I bet you have been told, time and time again, to be Quiet too. Inside though, you are craving something different, better, more aligned to your soul. You do not want to be Quiet anymore. You want to be Loud—to say what's on your mind without apology, to stop being afraid, and to live life on your terms.

You yearn to be a Loud Woman.

What is a Loud Woman? You may think it has to do with increased volume—and it could—but not always. Loudness is a state of mind. It's when a woman breaks the shackles that have kept her Quiet.

How have we been kept Quiet? Well, there's the literal translation of making less noise. In addition, societal conditioning has quieted us by teaching us to not trust ourselves, to always have good manners, and what behaviors we should tolerate from men.

"She's as quiet as a mouse" is an expression we hear all the time. Quiet girls are good girls, right? Quiet girls do not bother anyone.

They do not upset anyone. They do what's expected of them without complaint and with a smile.

Inside this quiet mouse of a girl, though, is a Loud Woman ready to break free.

Is this you? If so, you have come to the right place. I have taken what I have learned on my Loud Woman Journey and extracted lessons to help you on yours. You will break through your fear mindset and do things scared. You will learn to set up boundaries so people no longer take advantage of you. You will improve your self-worth so you can (finally) get the things you deserve. You will learn to trust yourself, because you are the expert at what's best for you.

And I will illuminate this path so you can join other women who are on the same journey, and we can love and support each other as the Loud Women we are.

This journey will not be easy, but I am here with my torch to light the way. Together, we will traverse out of our Quiet Caves into a new world, where women are Louder, happier, and more fulfilled; where the ripple effect of Loud Women will bring balance to our world; and where things improve for *all* humans.

The guys have been running the world for a long time. In many ways, they have done an outstanding job. In other ways, not so much. War, greed, wealth inequality, environmental issues—these are all byproducts of masculine leadership. At the heart of it all is a scarcity mindset that tells us there is not enough for everyone.

We know it's not true, though. God has given us plenty.

That's why, right now, we need feminine leadership. To do that, we need every woman to become a Loud Woman.

Loud Woman does not mean Super Woman. We will not be perfect on this journey, and you may feel like quitting. Please don't. We are here to change the world, and that means we must keep moving.

So, if you lose your footing, read this book. If you get skittish, read this book. If you become unsure, read this book. If you feel like there is no point, read this book.

Loud Woman, come with me. Our world is going to shit, and we can stop this tail spin if we rise up and get Louder.

It's time to stop being a Quiet Mouse and transform into a Loud Woman.

Are you ready?

WORTHY

Your crown has been bought and paid for. Put it on your head
and wear it.

— MAYA ANGELOU

STRANGLING

December 27, 1994. It's funny how I remember the exact date some twenty years later—the day my college sweetheart of three years broke up with me.

"I've met someone else," he explained. He plunged his hands deep into his front pockets as he leaned against the kitchen counter.

I stared at the wall over my stove in complete disbelief, feeling faint from the bomb he just dropped on me. I made my way to the edge of my sofa and asked him, "What did I do wrong?"

"Nothing," he said.

I tried to look him in the eyes, but he refused to meet my gaze. I didn't believe him. I began to sob, deep cries from the innermost parts of my soul. He turned around and left.

What did I do wrong? I kept asking myself, rocking back and forth on my couch.

I could not wrap my arms around the fact that my boyfriend—this sweet, good guy—had cheated on me. He always seemed as enamored of me as I was with him. In fact, I had just moved to his hometown three months before so I could be near him.

I must have made a mistake, somewhere, sometime, to make his heart turn against me.

As the tears poured down my face, I promised myself, right then and there, not to be one of *those* ex-girlfriends. I wanted nothing but happiness for my boyfriend—that's how much I loved him. If I couldn't bring him the happiness he deserved, so be it. I vowed I would not cuss him out or demand the details on why he cheated on me. Instead, I became obsessed with "keeping it classy." I was so focused on *his* feelings that I pushed down my need for closure and time to mourn.

I missed the companionship though. I just wanted to watch a movie from Blockbuster and cuddle with someone on the couch. Since I was sixteen years old, I always had a boyfriend. Suddenly, I was alone in a strange city, far from my family, and the loneliness amplified my heartbreak. I began to take extra care of appearance—even losing weight (that I didn't need to lose), curling my hair, and wearing more provocative clothing—all in an attempt to catch someone's eye.

It didn't work. I spent most of my evenings alone, unless I was working. I felt like I had a scarlet letter on my chest, but my letter was "L" for *loser*, signaling to the whole world how I couldn't keep my sweet boyfriend faithful to me.

I poured myself into my studies at the State University of West Georgia, where I worked toward my master's degree in history. I loved graduate school—the conversations, the research, and my professors. I had a perfect grade point average and a full-time assistantship. As a result of my hard work, my professors selected me for induction into an honor society. I was so thrilled. I remember buying a pretty skirt to wear to the induction ceremony, curling my long hair so it cascaded down my back.

After the ceremony, a bunch of us history students hung out at a picnic table outside. This is where my friend, Christina, introduced me to a guy with a beautiful smile and big, brown eyes. I'll call him Dale. We spoke about our history studies, and I learned he was finishing up his undergraduate degree to become a history teacher. We talked about Hootie and the Blowfish, and how awesome our professors were. I was struck by his intelligence and soft, Southern drawl. He asked me for my phone number, and I wrote it down for him.

He called me that night, and we spoke until 2 a.m. I can't remember what we spoke about, but I remember feeling relieved that a handsome, smart guy was interested in me. After a few phone calls, he asked me out. We lived about an hour apart from each other, so I suggested he come to my town, where we could have dinner and a movie. He agreed.

When he knocked on my apartment door, dressed in his Tommy Hilfiger shirt, my heart pounded in excitement. We enjoyed a wonderful dinner out, but decided to skip the movie and head back to my apartment to talk. While we chatted on the couch, Dale leaned in to kiss me. It was sweet, and as we kissed more, I quickly realized Dale was not an expert kisser. His shaved face rubbed my chin raw as he kept trying to kiss me tenderly. I found it endearing, but as he saw the red marks, he sat up and rubbed his brow. He told me he was embarrassed.

"I have something that will make you feel better!" I exclaimed. I went to my kitchen and dished out some ice cream into a bowl. I then sat back on the couch, next to Dale, and spoon-fed ice cream to him. He remained a little morose, but he began to relax more.

He looked into my eyes, and he said, "Would you ever go on a second date with me?"

"Of course," I replied, kissing him on the cheek. And I did. We dated for several weeks, and our romance blossomed. Several months later, I decided to move closer to the college, which also put me closer to Dale.

Shortly after moving into my apartment, the first sign occurred. As Dale installed a security device on my sliding glass door, he somehow shattered the interior pane of glass. Instead of just yelling "fuck" and moving on, he became almost despondent. I told him not to worry about it; the apartment complex probably would not even realize the second pane was gone. As I spoke, Dale sat on my sofa and stared ahead, not saying a word, like his world had shattered, instead of a piece of glass. I shrugged it off as someone who was deeply feeling.

My instincts, though, were firing off on all cylinders. Something was off. My instincts told me to run, but I hated being alone. For the most part, Dale was a really nice guy, so I continued the relationship.

Eventually, Dale spent more nights at my apartment than his home. That's when I learned he was obsessed with pornography. He had memorized the measurements of each *Playboy* Playmate of the Month for the preceeding three years. Our sex became a *required* nightly activity, even when I was menstruating. He always wanted me to do things to him sexually that made me uncomfortable, but I relented because I learned he had a temper.

His temper stayed at a slow boil at the beginning of our relationship. Once he moved in, I saw the full wrath of it. One time, I wanted to take a shower alone, but he didn't want me to. So, he turned off the breaker to the hot water heater and barricaded himself in the front of the bathroom door. Dale also cut me down intellectually, telling me I had a crappy education and didn't know as much as him. He also told me what to wear, insisting I layer my clothing with slips and camisoles to maintain my modesty. When Dale did not like what I wore, he ripped my clothes—just a little—so I could not wear that shirt or skirt again. As my live-in boyfriend, he only paid the electric bill (which wasn't much), yet told me I couldn't live without his financial contribution.

He was clever with his physical abuse, never leaving bruises or marks where people could see them. He pushed me down on to the sofa. He kept a hand on my chest. One time he squeezed hard on my upper arms. It was wintertime, so he knew no one would see those bruises.

If you asked me back then if Dale abused me, I would have said no because he never hit me in the face. I had defined physical abuse as when a guy hit a woman in the face only, not the arms, or chest, or back.

Why didn't I leave? I was afraid he would hurt me, those pushes and grips intensifying to punches to the face. He convinced me I could not live alone—both emotionally and financially. I worried he would stalk me, and I was afraid for my cat (he had hurt my first cat to the point where she had to be euthanized).

It just wasn't the bodily fear, though. I was scared of shattering my exterior image of a grounded, smart, independent woman—a feminist graduate from an all-women's college. Surely a woman like me could never be in an abusive relationship, right?

And I was scared that no one else would want me—that I was forever scarred now, so I might as well be grateful for the relationship I did have.

I tried to find the tenderness in him, and focused on those traits, telling myself he was a good guy with a bad temper. I thought he would grow out of it. At Christmas, he asked me to marry him, and I said yes because I was scared to say no. Dread became a way of life. I prayed marriage would soften him, but I also worried it wouldn't.

Dale had control of every aspect of my life, and though I did not see it at the time, he was an abuser on every level—emotionally, mentally, verbally, physically, and sexually. I used to fanaticize about being rescued by other men. I would pray my college boyfriend would dump his girlfriend and come find me. I wondered how I could discretely tell a police officer acquaintance about my abuse, so he could help me get Dale out. I sent telepathic messages to my dad, hoping he would mysteriously show up at my doorstep.

One cold January morning, I woke up early to work on my master's thesis. I had been working on it *hard* for days, neglecting my appearance. So, I decided to do my hair and make-up, and put some decent clothes on, thinking Dale would appreciate it. When Dale woke up, he demanded to know why I was "dressed up," and before I could tell him, he clutched his hands around my neck, squeezing his fingers, while simultaneously pushing me down on the sofa.

I can't breathe.

Oh my God, he's strangling me.

Usually when Dale engaged in physical behavior, he doubled down on his reasons and maintained his temper level.

As soon as Dale steered me to the sofa, though, I saw a different look in his eyes—one of fear and regret. Dale crossed an indisputable line. He immediately let go of my neck, and put his head in my lap, tears streaming.

"I am so sorry, Jill. So sorry. I won't do it again," he cried.

In that moment, I saw my opportunity. I grabbed my keys and left.

I headed to the bank, intent on withdrawing all of my money to buy a plane ticket home. As I sat in the bank parking lot, I sobbed. I cried for the Jill that had gotten herself into this mess. I cried for my lack of rescuers. I cried because I knew that running home—without a bag packed or my cat in a safe place—was not the answer.

It was then that Dale called me on my car phone. He apologized again. I heard his remorse, and realized it was my chance, probably my last one, to get out of this relationship with my safety intact. As I listened to his sobs and apologies, I devised a plan. First, I needed him to move out. Once he was out and safely away from me, I could end our relationship.

I looked in the rearview mirror. The eye make-up I had so carefully applied that morning was gone; my eyes now swollen and puffy from tears and fear. Those eyes showed something else, though. A spark. That brave Jill was still in there. It was then I realized that the only person who could rescue me was myself.

I told Dale I would come back to my apartment on one condition: He must leave and not stay there. I positioned it as a "fresh start," a way to find ourselves in our relationship again. We would date and have fun. He liked the idea—probably out of desperation—and when I arrived back home, he and his packed duffel bag weren't there.

Within one hour, I went from being nearly strangled to feeling relieved and free. I used to kid myself that his attempted strangulation was the best thing that happened in our relationship. In all that horribleness, in that feeling of true bodily fear, I found a glimmer of hope.

It took four months for me to feel safe enough to break up with Dale. I did it over the phone after I had changed the locks on my apartment door. When my co-worker noticed I was not wearing my engagement ring, she hugged me and told me that I would be okay. I think she knew something was not right with my relationship.

I took a pause in my graduate program, partly because I needed a mental break, but mostly because I did not want to run into Dale on campus. I worked on my thesis on my own time and got a full-time job. I was not interested in dating anyone either. I relished being alone. I had never felt so free. I was living life on my own terms.

As I sat in my apartment, the scene of so much abuse, I realized this: *I am worthy of love, safety, kindness, and respect.* My past relationships do not define me. I get to do that—on my own terms and in the highest self-worth. That's what I deserved all along. It took being alone to realize it.

HIGH SELF-WORTH

I take a nap every day for two hours.

Yep, you read that correctly.

How do I pull this off? The short answer is this: *I know I deserve a two-hour nap.*

Trust me: I didn't always feel this way. When I napped in the past, I felt guilty about it. Shouldn't I be hanging out with my kids? Shouldn't I be working? Shouldn't I be cleaning the bathroom?

Those "shoulds" banged around in my head, and sometimes, I gave in to them. This resulted in a very cranky Jill.

I needed the rest, for sure. But what my soul really wanted was the solitude that comes with laying on my comfy bed for two hours. No worries, no obligations—just me and my pillow.

It's pure heaven.

I used to announce "I'm taking a nap!" to my household, as if I was asking permission. But I didn't need anyone's permission but my own. Now I just walk in my bedroom and close the door. Sometimes, I run. The solitude is worth the jaunt.

My guilt-free napping is a result of high self-worth. What does that mean, exactly? High self-worth is the value you place on yourself— from your intelligence to emotional health, to finances and your part of a relationship. Having high self-worth means you believe you are worth it—unapologetically and without explanation.

Here's how high self-worth can show up in a Loud Woman's life:

- Demand fair compensation;
- Do not give up easily, especially when conflict arises;
- Do not settle;
- Know you are worthy of healthy relationships;
- Put your needs first; and
- Enjoy guilt-free self-care.

Our current society grants us some worth in the home and as mothers, but only in certain circumstances. We are lauded for our exceptional housekeeping and home management skills, our decorating and cooking prowess, and our ability to juggle marriage, kids, and household demands. But if we pop anti-depressants or don't cook every night, people began to wonder.

We are valued as mothers too, as long as we look like we have our shit together. Make no mistake: We are valued for our uteruses, but not for our ability to make decisions about our uteruses.

Because society puts restrictions on our self-worth, I have devoted a whole section to improving your self-worth. Loud Women know if you wait for society to elevate your self-worth, you will be waiting until you take your final breath.

Increasing your self-worth will have an amazing ripple effect on other areas of your life. High self-worth improves your relationships, careers and businesses, checking accounts, health, and mindset. If you feel you are "worth" more in these areas, but are not getting what you deserve, then it's time to work on your self-worth.

No matter how old you are, you will have a lot to unravel when it comes to improving your self-worth. Your past relationships, former jobs, societal programming, and mindset will need to be analyzed and reset. Please don't let this scare you because it is important, necessary work. Furthermore, you will love the results because you will feel empowered. Let's get to it.

LOW SELF-WORTH

M y youngest son became a football player when he turned six, and he didn't stop playing until his senior year in high school.

This also meant that football was a part of my life too. I would drive him to practices and games, sign him up for football camps, and sacrifice my needs so I could afford new cleats or whatever equipment he needed.

I didn't mind: I loved being a football mom. I wore the team T-shirt and cheered from the stands. The team's victories felt like my own.

When my son was a junior in high school, he would head straight to the locker room after each game. The other kids would wait for their parents, take pictures, and talk about the game. Every game, my husband and I would walk on the field, hoping to catch Joe before he headed to the locker room, but he never looked for us.

I am sure my son didn't mean anything by it, but his actions broke my heart. Football was my journey too. I just wanted a few minutes with him after each game—just like it had been since he started playing football in kindergarten.

That's why, when my son came home from practice on the night before his first game as a senior, he found a letter from me on his bed.

In my letter, I shared how proud I was of his tenacity, determination, and teamwork. I reminisced about how long his "football career" had been and expressed my hope that he looks back with fond memories.

Then, I wrote this:

You probably don't realize this, but your football journey has been a journey for Dad and me, too. Think about all the practices we took you to, all the games we traveled to, all the camps we sent you to. Remember how Dad coached many of your teams—often taking up most evenings and weekends. It's been our pleasure to be part of your football life, and when your season ends, our football journey will end too.

That's why I want you to stay on the field after each game, and wait for Dad and me. Please do not go straight to the locker room. We have been on this football journey—together—and we will stop this journey together, too.

I should have said this to Joe during his junior year, but I didn't want a conflict. Managing the emotions and expectations of a teenage boy is like navigating a mine field. Truth be told: I wanted to avoid a conflict, but in doing so, I dismissed my self-worth as a parent. Didn't I deserve a few post-game words and maybe a hug?

Joe read my note, and after every game (all twelve of them), he waited for Richard and me. He often didn't say much, but he indulged us with a short conversation and pictures. My heart filled with gratitude—not just for Joe, but for having enough self-worth to ask for what I needed.

∿

Before we get into analyzing and resetting our self-worth, let's take a deeper dive into how low self-worth shows up.

Think about the times you have put yourself last, particularly when you did not want to, but felt it was easier, safer, and less of a conflict to do so. This bubbles up in many places in my life, such as:

- Staying in abusive relationships;
- The division of household chores;
- Negotiating a car loan; and
- Having an office with a door.

See the range here? Low self-worth permeated in situations from dangerous (abusive relationships) to financial (negotiating a car loan).

Right now, list the times you have put yourself last, reluctantly. This may be a long list because one thing's for sure: Women are excellent at self-sacrificing.

Once you have your list, look for themes—certain hot spots in your life when you were miserable because you put yourself last. Those are the areas you want to work on first.

Sometimes, you do not even realize you have low self-worth about something until someone points it out, or you are out of the situation and can reflect.

I learn self-worth lessons from reflection all the time. For example, when I began my coaching business in 2014, I had years of marketing experience and had been coaching my social media clients through my agency. None of this mattered, though, when I established my coaching prices.

I set my initial coaching prices low because I had this rationale: *No one will pay more because I have a newly formed coaching business.*

Huge mistake. I may have just opened my coaching business, but I did not consider my experience in marketing, as well as the work I have done with past clients. Furthermore, I did not consider the results my clients would receive from working with me. My clients were attracting more clients in their business, easily paying for their coaching investment within days.

I saw other marketing coaches charging more, so I felt like shit because I had to keep my prices low because I was "new" to the industry.

Do you see the bullshit I was feeding myself? I could not detach from the idea that a new coaching business equaled low prices. This is a self-worth problem. Deepening the issue were my fear of rejection and conflict because I was afraid someone would call me out for charging as much as my peers. *Who do you think you are?* I imagined them saying to me. (By the way, my Ego made this conversation up. The chances of it happening were slim to none—and who cares if it did. I see that now, of course.)

After a few months of bottom-feeder pricing, I asked my mentor what I should do, and she insisted I raise my prices immediately. I knew she was right and that's what I needed, but the idea scared me—all because I could not convince myself to charge based on my worth.

Sometimes you have to bargain with your Ego and take baby steps out of your comfort zone. That's what I did. I raised my price just slightly. Sure enough, none of my clients balked. *Whew, that wasn't so hard,* I thought.

After that initial price increase, I made a deal with myself: I would sell three more packages at the new price and then raise my price again. And after selling an additional three packages, I would bump up my price some more.

Admittedly, this was the scenic route to getting the compensation I deserved, but it got the job done. I would sell three, raise the price, sell another three, and raise the price. With each sale, I grew in confidence. My self-worth got higher; so high, in fact, that it drowned out my now-screaming Ego voice.

If you had told me I had low self-worth while I was going through this, I would have laughed at you. *No way!* I am a smart and intelligent woman with advanced degrees and a business. I have incredible self-worth.

See how I tied self-worth to my accomplishments? Sure, accomplishments can make you feel good, but they are external factors. To achieve high self-worth, you need to work on the internal stuff.

That's why I want you to reflect because hindsight is a powerful teacher. We are thankful for the lessons because that's how we improve our self-worth. To glean these lessons, though, we have to look back.

Once you acknowledge where low self-worth has occurred in your life, then you can start the journey on improving your self-worth. Notice I said *journey*. Improving your self-worth will take time. Think of it as a slow boat ride across the ocean. With every situation you learn about and improve upon, you will propel your boat across the sea. Throughout your journey, you will look back and be amazed at the milestones you have accomplished. Hand in hand, you will feel frustrated. The biggest frustration? Getting others to buy into your self-worth too. That's where your tenacity will kick in. Trust me: Your self-worth and tenacity are intricately linked. Together, these two forces will merge in ways you did not think possible.

Here's what I want you to know, you are worth it. You are worth everything you want in your life. The journey may suck and you may feel like giving up, but do not. Your life will improve in a hundred different ways by improving your self-worth. If you need to, write "I am worth it!" on a Post-It Note and stick it to your bathroom mirror or refrigerator. Keep saying this affirmation in your head, because every word is true. *You are worth it. You are worth it. You are worth it.*

NO MEDAL FOR 'GREAT SACRIFICER'

O ver my desk is a collection of medals.
I have medals for completing 5K races, 8K races, 10K races, and virtual races. Some medals have yellow ribbons; others have red. One of my medals is shaped like a sneaker (for the Thin Mint 5K, sponsored by the Girl Scouts); another is shaped like a Storm Trooper (for the Star Wars Dark Side 5K). Each medal tells a story—one of perseverance, pride, and sweat.

What you will never see on my medal display is one for "Great Sacrificer." You would think with my past life choices that I was striving for such a medal, collecting moments where I put myself last like miles on my Apple Watch. Despite my sacrifices, I will never get a Great Sacrificer medal because it doesn't exist. But damn, you think one does by the way many women act.

Self-sacrificing is not noble. When you lie on your death bed, you will think about your regrets. How many of your regrets will be tied to sacrifices? Will you regret what you did not do, like taking care of yourself more, or going on that trip, or making that career switch?

You know the answer. Thankfully, you are still alive and there's no time like the present.

Do not strive to receive a non-existent "Greatest Sacrificer" award.

I know we are surrounded by messages to sacrifice our happiness for others, but it's a farce—an extension of our patriarchal societal conditioning keeps us from playing a bigger game. People in power need us to sacrifice because that's how they stay in power. Do not fall for it.

I especially see this with moms. Moms sacrificing their "me" time; moms sacrificing their careers; moms sacrificing their health; moms sacrificing physical space in their home. It happens so often, we do not even realize it. To give up something feels so natural and right. But I beg of you: Why should we always be sacrificing for the benefit of others? Because society says so?

No longer, Loud Woman.

Let's create a new medal—one that's about living life on your terms, demanding what you deserve, and having no regrets. We can call it the Loud Woman Medal.

The first step in acquiring the Loud Woman medal is to improve your self-worth. If you do not think you deserve something, you won't obtain it, right? That's why you must boost your self-worth. When you feel worthy and deserving, you will fight like hell to get it.

Loud Women are a scrappy bunch. When a Loud Woman has her sights set on something, she will get it. So, let's make a pledge to go for it. Demand what you want. Ignore the internal and external pressure to constantly sacrifice for the betterment of others. You deserve to be happy. You deserve to live life on your own terms. The Loud Woman Medal is yours—reach out and take it.

GIFTS

I wanted to be a teacher since I was a little girl. I had a small blue chalkboard that I propped on my window sill, and every day after school, I would pretend to be my teacher and rehash what I learned that day. I'd go over spelling words and word problems, using my textbooks and workbooks to help me teach. I'd write math equations on the chalk board, showing my imaginary students how to "carry the one." I loved the feel of yellow chalk on my fingers (I still do).

When I went to college, I declared English Education as my major. The thought of teaching high schoolers about the joy of writing and literature burned inside me. It did not take long, however, for me to shift my goal a bit. After being exposed to college faculty, I decided to teach at a college level. This took me to graduate school where I was a teacher's assistant. I loved academia because the conversations seemed so important, and I appreciated how the professors challenged me to think about different perspectives. I wanted to do that with my students, too. After only being in my master's degree program a few months, I began to think ahead about where I'd like to get my Ph.D.

About two years into my graduate studies, I got scared. I was in the abusive relationship with Dale, and his verbal assault on my intelligence took its toll. I never felt worthy enough, despite my full scholarship and high-grade point average. With those messages blasting in my head, I looked around at my brilliant fellow grad students and equally brilliant faculty, and thought: *I do not measure up.*

For my master's thesis, I wrote about the education of Wesleyan College students in the early years of the college's history. Many education scholars dismiss Southern women's colleges as finishing schools. While that may be true of some of the first women's colleges, that was not the case for Wesleyan. As I proved in my thesis, Wesleyan's early curriculum was robust and advanced, equal to many of the comparable men's colleges.

It took me three years to research and write my thesis. On a crisp October morning, I defended it to the three professors who made up my thesis committee. We sat in a classroom right down the hall from the history department's offices—where I had spent so much time. My thesis advisors challenged me on my proposal and forced me to take a stand. After defending my thesis, they asked me to wait outside while they deliberated. It only took them a few minutes to ask me to come back into the classroom to announce their decision.

"Congratulations, Jill! You have successfully defended your thesis!" exclaimed Dr. Kenneth Noe, my major thesis professor. He then encouraged me to publish my thesis in a historical journal. The other professors asked where I was applying for my Ph.D.

I sheepishly listened and thanked them for their votes of confidence. But I had already made up my mind: My academic career was done. Why? Because I had decided I was not good enough to teach at a college level. In fact, I decided that I would never be a teacher at any level. Game over.

We are born with Divine Gifts. Some of us can sing, play an instrument, write, or draw. Others of us are gifted athletes, natural-born chess players, or limber dancers. And others of us can communicate with animals, read Tarot cards, or trance channel with a spirit higher than ourselves.

Our Divine Gifts are numerous and varied. What's one Divine Gift is not the other's. Despite the difference of our Gifts, what we have in common is this: We are divinely gifted.

These Gifts are innate. I envision God depositing them into our souls with a smile. It's our job, as humans, to identify our Gifts, practice to improve them, and use them to make the world a better place. It does not matter if it's a talent to play tennis or to illustrate cartoons, these talents are Gifts for us to use, over and over again.

Some of us use our Gifts professionally—as an employee or entrepreneur. Others of us use our Gifts as a hobby, side gig, or for self-care. There is no right or wrong way to share our Gifts, but share them we must. That's what Loud Women do.

My Divine Gift is to teach. And while at the end of my graduate studies I may have decided to never teach, I didn't realize my Divine Gift would never be squelched. I was like a dormant volcano. My Divine Gift was at my core, sending out tremors to remind me it's there. Sometimes, I would feel it bubbling inside of me. I would often wonder, *what if...*

As I began my corporate career, I trained new employees. I taught marketing to senior management teams. I explained how to do something, and then cheered my colleagues on. I could still feel this love of teaching, but I stayed in my "doing" roles and convinced myself it is where I belonged.

This pattern continued even when I opened my first business. I settled on being the "doer," the one who implemented social media instead of teaching it. While doing the work was okay, what made my heart sing was teaching my clients—from explaining why we should implement a certain strategy, to teaching them how to implement a task themselves.

It was not until 2013—sixteen years after graduating with my master's degree—that I finally allowed myself to share my Gifts as a marketing coach. Professional coaching certainly involved teaching, and I finally began to feel more fulfilled. As my confidence grew, I stopped calling myself a "marketing coach" because it did not explain what I did. *I was a marketing teacher.* As I began to identify as one, my

Ego piped up to try to stop me. Messages like *who do you think you are,* and *you are a hack,* and *real teachers would be insulted* all played full blast in my head.

Thankfully, I ignored my mind chatter. How? I reminded myself that my Divine Gift is to teach. I knew it as a six-year-old with yellow chalk dust on her fingers, and I knew it again as a forty-something woman. When I was teaching, I was on fire—like I was doing something so innate and effortless, as if I was born to do it. I also knew I was changing people's lives for the better.

I loved sharing knowledge so my clients could make better, more confident marketing decisions. What I most loved, though, were the pep talks, the challenges I threw down, and the truth telling. Knowledge is power, for sure, but if you do not have the courage or confidence to do something with that knowledge, it will die like fruit on a vine.

Look back at your favorite teachers. I bet they filled you with knowledge; I also bet they believed in you, inspired you, and held you to a higher standard. Furthermore, they had faith in you when you did not.

These teacherly gifts? I have them. Even though it took me a while to get here, I am now sharing my Gifts and changing lives.

Unfortunately for many women, ignoring or downplaying our Gifts is commonplace. Why? The list is endless and as unique as our Gifts: fear of what others may say, feeling like you cannot make a living from it, Imposter Syndrome, putting yourself last. All of these reasons really boil down to the main one: Low self-worth.

To share your Gifts fully and unapologetically is an extension of high self-worth. This is beautiful in two ways. First, when you fully own and share your Gifts, you are so fulfilled. You can feel a happy buzz in your soul. It feels so good, and you deserve to feel this good!

Second, as you share your Gifts, you create a ripple effect. You help people, and yes, raising their self-worth as a result. It does not matter what your Gifts are, you will create a ripple effect. You're a yoga instructor? Your ripple effect is the good health your student now has after taking your classes. You're a bad-ass seamstress? Your ripple effect is how you make someone confident in her clothes so she can nail that job interview. When you share your Gifts, you are sending out these lovely ripples that make others feel better. And what happens when they feel better? They have higher self-worth and create their own ripple effects.

Truth-telling time: If you are not embracing and sharing your Gifts, you are being stingy. Yes, you read that correctly. You are depriving yourself of the happiness and fulfillment you deserve. You are not helping people, which stops the ripple effect. If our world is to find itself in a better place, it's because Loud Women like you and me are out there sharing our Divine Gifts.

You know what your Divine Gifts are. You may have to get quiet and listen for that little voice, but it's there. As a Loud Woman, disregard what your Ego is telling you (or what others are telling you) and tune into that quiet voice who says, *You are meant to do this.* And then do it. Loud Woman, it's time.

ASK AND PERSIST

P ets teach us so much about being better humans. Case in point:
My orange tabby cat, Jane.

Jane may only be restricted to meows, but that doesn't stop her from telling you what she wants.

If she wants in a bedroom, she will meow at the door and hit the doorknob with her paws until someone lets her in. If she wants to eat, she'll meow while leading you to the kitchen. And if she wants her feline brother to stop messing with her, she'll hiss and pull her ears back.

There is no mistaking what Janie wants because she will tell you. Loudly.

I could learn a lesson or two from Janie. I can't count the times I have not expressed what I want.

How about you?

High self-worth means you ask for what you want, and you do not give up until you get it. This touches on two skills Loud Women must have: sharing *exactly* what you want or need, and not giving up if you did not get it right away.

Let's say you want your husband to unload the dishwasher. In your head, you hope he just does it without you asking. You may even send him telepathic messages. Time passes and the dishwasher sits full, so one of two things may happen: You finally break down and ask him to do it (and he takes his time, pissing you off even more), or you get mad that he didn't read your mind, and you empty the dishwasher yourself.

Isn't it funny how we can ask in our heads, but when it comes time to use our mouths, we don't?

Others cannot read your mind. Not to mention, most people need clear direction. We know this, yet we still do not speak up. Why?

In her book, *13 Things Mentally Strong Women Don't Do*, Amy Morin referenced a 2014 Harvard study about job salaries and advertisements. If the ad mentioned the salary was negotiable, women would negotiate. If the ad said the salary was not negotiable, women did not broach the subject (even though the men in the study did).

"Imagine how much money women might be leaving on the table because they don't dare to broach the subject," Morin writes. "Think of all the other things women might miss out on simply because they don't try."[1]

Why don't we ask for what we want, and why don't we persist when we do not get it right away?

Here are some reasons:

- Fear of rejection;
- Fear of being ignored;
- Don't want to be told it's not what you want;
- Someone will laugh at you;
- You don't want to be a burden;
- You don't want to look weak or give off the impression that you do not have your act together;
- It's easier or faster to do it yourself;
- You might actually get what you want; or
- You feel like people should just know without you asking.

Often these fears and beliefs are extensions of low self-worth, meaning you do not feel deserving. This comes from your Ego, who wants to keep you safe and secure. Opening your mouth to ask for what you want puts you in scary territory—places like rejection, teasing, and negligence.

Here's the humdinger: *When you do not ask, you never get what you want.* Doing everything yourself is unfair and leads to burn-out.

My favorite story about asking and persisting is one you have probably heard before: "Nevertheless, she persisted" featuring Senator Elizabeth Warren of Massachusetts.

in 2017, President Donald Trump nominated Senator Jeff Sessions to be U.S. Attorney General. Sessions had a troubled past, specifically when it came to racism. During the nomination process, Senator Warren wanted to read a letter by Coretta Scott King about Sessions. The letter was written in 1986 when Sessions was Attorney General for the Southern District of Alabama. As Warren started to read it, she was told not to by Republican leaders. She persisted, though, which lead to Senate Republicans voting to rebuke Warren for violating Senate Rule No. 19, which says Senators cannot "directly or indirectly, by any form of words, impute to another Senator or to other Senators any conduct or motive unworthy or unbecoming a Senator."[2]

With this vote, Warren could not speak for the rest of the nomination debate.

When justifying Warren's barring, McConnell explained she would not cease reading the letter after being told to stop. "Nevertheless, she persisted," he said, unknowingly coining a feminist phrase that's still popular today.

Did they succeed in silencing Elizabeth Warren? Not one bit. After leaving the Senate Chamber, she jumped on Facebook Live and read King's letter. She got what she wanted, even if it did not look like what she intended. Nevertheless, she persisted.

Interesting side note: After Warren was booted out of the debate, three of her male colleagues were able to read the same Coretta Scott King letter—without rebuke. It was only when a female Senator wanted to read it that it was a problem. Sexism is alive and well in our Senate Chambers, unfortunately.

I share Senator Warren's story to inspire you. During the entire ordeal, she was specific about what she wanted—to read King's letter, which she felt was important to include in a debate about the future U.S. Attorney General. She was told no, but she knew this letter was important, so she persisted. She did so without apology—and never gave up—even after she was kicked out for her persistence.

Now you may read this story and think: *Well, this is what happens when you persist! You get silenced!* But did she really get silenced? Absolutely not. She ended up reading the letter on Facebook Live, which was probably watched by more people than in the Congressional debate. She did not stop until her message was heard, even if it meant changing *how* it was heard.

Women need to take a page from Warren's playbook. If she can ask for what she wants and persists until she gets it, in an environment steeped with blatant sexism, we can do the same in our homes, jobs, and relationships.

What fuels Warren's drive? Her high self-worth. She knew she deserved time to read King's letter and never backed down from it.

Just like Warren, you deserve whatever you want too. And just like Warren, you will get it if you ask for it and persist until you get it. Banish the Ego talk that it's easier to do it yourself, or that you will be ignored, or that someone will reject your ask. True, these things could happen, but none of them are the end of the world.

Add a little optimism instead. Tell yourself: *I receive what I ask for* and *I am persistent in getting what I deserve.* Saying these affirmations in your head, over and over again, will calm your Ego and bring out your inner Loud Woman.

Like with everything, this will not happen overnight, but you must start somewhere to get the ball rolling. Right now, think about something small you want. Maybe it's your husband unloading the dishwasher. Maybe it's having your son take the trash out to the curb. Maybe it's giving yourself permission to join that yoga class. Whatever it is, start there. Yes, your Ego may holler at you but persist.

Remember Elizabeth Warren on the Senate floor, trying to read an important letter, and the persistence she mustered to eventually read it, and be inspired by it.

Loud Women ask for what they want and don't give up until they get it. That includes you.

9

SETTLING

For five years, I was a marketing manager for a large hospital system, and I was ready for change. And not just any change—a promotion. My employer had hand-picked me, out of hundreds of eligible managers, to join a "succession planning" track. Essentially, this track prepared me for a promotion and gave me an edge should a director position open up.

After months and months of waiting, my employer posted a director position I was qualified for. I applied and was interviewed. The interview went great—I was on fire—and I knew I put my best foot forward. Unfortunately, the vice president was not interested in hiring internal talent and filled the position with an external candidate. I was gutted. Wasn't I suppose to have an advantage as a "succession planning" candidate? What else could I have done to make myself a worthier candidate? I didn't ask or complain, though, feeling it wouldn't do any good. The decision was made, and I moved on.

Then, a manager position opened up. Even though it would not be a promotion, it would be something different and would pay more because I would have a larger team under me. I was more than qualified for this position, too, so I decided to throw my hat in the ring. Once again, my vice president chose an external candidate for the job.

He didn't tell me why I didn't get the position, just that he liked "fresh ideas" from external candidates. In hindsight, I should have complained to Human Resources, but I bit my tongue, not wanting to rock the boat.

The vice president liked my tenacity, I guess, and offered me a web site coordinator position, under the very manager who got the job I wanted. He elevated the pay of the position so I would keep the same pay. However, I would lose my office, team, and manager title. I would gain, however, valuable experience and a change of pace.

So, here I was: A manager who was ready for a promotion with only one offer on the table, and it was a demotion.

I took the coordinator position. I regret it to this day because I settled. I kept quiet about the hiring choices being made around me. I did not lean into my self-worth.

Why did I settle? When I look back at it now, I was afraid to argue with my new vice president and too tired to persist (applying for two jobs and not getting them zapped my energy). The coordinator position felt better than no job, and I believed I would learn new things and be offered a manager job in the future.

Well, I did learn a lot, but not what I expected. I learned what it was like to be part of a team that backstabbed you and made you the subject of mean gossip. Office politics hung around me like a smelly wet blanket. My normal cheerful disposition vanished, and I began to yell at my co-workers at meetings.

I settled, and I was miserable. Six months later, I could not bear it anymore and quit my job. My co-workers bought me a cake and sent me off, and I never looked back.

Loud Women do not settle. As you ask for what you want and persist in achieving it, you will confront scenarios where it will be tempting to settle.

For example, if you want a pay raise, and your employer instead offers you an office with a window, accepting that office is settling.

While an office with a window is nice, it does not equal higher pay, and it's not what you deserve.

Oftentimes, women settle because they do not want to persist anymore. I get it: Persistence is exhausting. Persistence can lead to conflict, which women openly avoid, and it can wreak havoc on your mindset.

The truth? When we settle, we regret it. We are unhappier than when we started. Sure, you can have a nice office with a window, but when you look at your direct deposit and feel undervalued, your self-worth plummets.

Settling is a form of giving up. It's a message of *I am not worthy of what I want*. In fact, settling is worse than not speaking up at all. Why? Because you will be more upset after you settle than if you stayed quiet.

Do not settle. Do not give up. You are worthy of everything you want and everything you need. Tap into your self-worth when settling becomes a temptation, and remember why you asked in the first place.

I wish I had. If I could do this scenario again, I would have fought harder for my promotion. I would have alerted Human Resources about the vice president's hiring practices and began looking for a new job outside of the company. I would remember why I deserved to be treated more fairly.

The journey will not be easy, but if you settle, the journey gets harder. Always remember: Loud Women do not settle because we deserve only the best.

10

COMPENSATION

I was sitting in the bleachers at my son's football game when I overheard a woman scoff at the idea of pay inequity. "Businesses hire based on ability and skills, not sex!" I have no idea where that comment came from, but I do know this: Despite her adamancy, she was wrong.

In the U.S., women of all races make less per hour than their male counterparts for the same work. According to the U.S. Census Bureau, who reported this data in 2018, for every dollar a white male earns working full-time:

- A white woman earns 80%;
- A black woman earns 66%; and
- A Hispanic woman earns 58%. [3]

Have kids? Full-time working fathers receive about $141 more a week than a man without children. However, women with or without children make the same. [4]

And promotions? A Lean-In Survey polled 329 companies with more than thirteen million employees, and only one in five of these companies had women at the C-level. [5]

And raises? Harvard Business Review cites than only 15% of women get requested raises, versus 20% of men. [6]

I wish I had these facts on hand when I heard that woman declare that pay inequity does not exist. Clearly, it does. While other countries ensure women are paid the same as men, American women stay behind.

If you need further proof, look no further than the U.S. Women's Soccer Team (USWNT). They have been fighting for pay equity and equal treatment for years. In 2016, the USWNT player leadership group filed a complaint over the disparity in pay and treatment as compared to the U.S. men soccer players. This complaint was replaced by a lawsuit filed by all twenty-eight members of the USWNT on March 28, 2020.

Their lawsuit breaks down the pay disparity:

- A top U.S. women's soccer player makes 38% of what a top U.S. men's soccer player earns—to the tune of a $164,320 pay gap.
- If the U.S. women's soccer team won twenty non-tournament games, their top players would earn a maximum of $99,000. Their male counterpart would earn an average of $262,320 for doing the same thing. That's a $163,320 pay gap.
- The 2014 World Cup Men's soccer team earned $5.375 million in bonuses and was eliminated in the sixteenth round. A year later, when the U.S. women won their World Cup, they only received $1.725 million. That's a $3.65 million gap. [7]

Not only were the women asking for equal pay, they wanted back pay. An economics expert hired by USWNT said U.S. Soccer owed these women about $66 million in damages. [8]

So, why the pay disparity? U.S. Soccer's official answer was that "market realities" do not justify equal pay for these women athletes. In other words, the women's soccer team does not produce the same revenue as men. Additionally, they cite that the men's and women's contracts are negotiated separately and these two teams have different compensation models. [9]

In their lawsuit, the women refuted U.S. Soccer's claim that women's soccer did not produce the same revenue or viewership as the men's soccer team. The 2015 Women's World Cup title was the most-watched soccer game in the history of the sport in the U.S. The women also played more games per year and trained more than the U.S. Men's Soccer Team (USMNT). [8] Clearly, they are bringing in revenue and viewers—and doing it better than the men's team.

The *real* reason for the pay disparity was revealed in a claim U.S. Soccer made in the 2020 lawsuit, when they said "it is undisputed that the job of [Men's National Team] player requires materially more strength and speed than the job of [Women's National Team] player." It also added that "the job of USMNT players carries more responsibility than the job of a USWNT player."[10]

Oh, hey there, sexism! We knew you were there all along.

When this statement found its way to the press, then U.S Soccer President Carlos Cordeiro issued an apology, but soccer players like Megan Rapinoe were not having it. "[The court filing] was pretty similar to what we've heard before." [11]

Despite the evidence, a federal judge threw out important parts of the women's lawsuit, including their low pay claims and unequal work conditions. The U.S. Women's soccer team have appealed these decisions. [12]

Ashlyn Harris, a member of the USWNT and one of the claimants in the lawsuit, said in an August 2020 article in *Allure Magazine* that, "What really moves a lot of us is changing the conversation, the culture. You're playing for more than the popularity of the sport. You're playing to impact people's lives across all industries. We're trying to empower people to feel strong enough to stand for something that is important to them. And right now, for us, that is pay equity." [13]

Make no mistake: The equal pay fight by the U.S. Women's Soccer team is every woman's fight. The sexism behind determining women's wages is now front and center for all the world to see, thanks to these Loud Women. And when they win their fight (because they will), their victory will have a tremendous ripple effect for all women workers.

Loud Woman, it's time for you to demand fair compensation, too. You are worthy of getting paid the same as your male colleagues. The idea that men should get paid more because they cannot get pregnant, or because they are breadwinners, are grossly outdated, and honestly, these factors should not matter. You should be compensated for the job you do at work—not what's happening at home.

And if you're an entrepreneur, you are not off the hook either. I have helped countless female entrepreneurs with their pricing mindset. Most feel like they need to charge less or worry about raising their prices. Their reasons? They do not feel they can charge more because of their "lack of experience," or they think their customers will not pay a higher price. These are all untruths, told to us by our Ego and perpetuated by society. Your price should be determined by the results your clients receive, not your experience.

If you are accepting less than you deserve, then you are settling. And you are settling because of low self-worth. You have to believe you are worthy of fair compensation, or you will never receive it. When thinking about why you should be compensated, stop working in a lack mindset: "I don't have the college degree," or "I don't have the experience." None of this matters if you have been hired to do the job. What *does* matter is your ability to do the job. Are you doing the job well? Are you meeting or exceeding the expectations for your job? Then yes, you deserve to be compensated fairly for it. Once you can wrap your head around this fact, you will feel more confident in demanding fair compensation.

Pay equity is a hard fight. You will feel like quitting. Your Ego will pipe up messages of low self-worth in your head, and you will probably hear it from your boss, Human Resources, or some random lady who thinks that pay inequity is not a thing. Push past these remarks and let your high self-worth motivate you.

Take a page from the U.S. Women's soccer team. They know they are worthy of a pay increase. They have the data to prove it, but more importantly, they *believe it* with every cell of their bodies. That's why they keep fighting. That's why they file complaints, lawsuits, and appeals. They have their eye on the prize. Just like they work together to win Olympic Gold Medals and World Cups, they will not stop until they obtain their goal: to get paid the same as the men. Loud Women demand fair compensation. The U.S. Women's soccer team deserves it —and so do you.

11

RELATIONSHIPS

I opened this section with my story of a past abusive relationship. This is the first time I have ever told this story. I feel scared and vulnerable sharing it, but I am glad I did.

While I learned a lot of lessons from this abusive relationship, I am still struggling with high self-worth when it comes to relationships.

It's been years since this traumatic relationship ended, but the remnants are still around me. It's easy to believe the voice that got you in the traumatic relationship.

After I broke up with Dale, I took some time to be alone, which helped me heal because I learned what I liked about myself and what I wanted in a partner. I often would sit in my apartment, rocking out to grunge music, and relishing the freedom I had to make my own choices, do what I want, and be who I wanted to be. This was a therapeutic time, for sure, but it also was one of self-discovery. My biggest discovery was this: I deserved a happy, fulfilling relationship.

A few months later, I met my husband, Richard, and he checked off all the boxes: Smart, honest, funny, gentle, and respectful. With him, not only did I not have to worry about being abused, I could share my thoughts with him, and he would listen.

Richard and I have been together since 1997. Is our marriage perfect? Absolutely not. But I firmly believe what keeps us together is our commitment to be respectful of each other's thoughts.

Despite the longevity of our relationship, the voice that got me into my relationship with Dale is still there. When I hear that voice, I tend to overreact and feel sorry for myself.

I have come to accept that this voice may never go away, so I have stopped fighting it. Instead, I work on strengthening another voice—that of my inner Loud Woman.

I want to talk to you about fortifying your Loud Woman voice around relationships, too.

For the purposes of this discussion, I am referring to romantic relationships and friendships. Relationships are all around us, for sure—from the relationship with a parent to the one with our co-workers. Please know I am not diminishing these relationships. If you can find healthy relationships with your lover and friends, you will have the self-worth skills to improve all of your relationships. No matter what relationship you are trying to improve, you must know one thing: *You must believe you deserve a healthy relationship.* That all starts with high self-worth.

For romantic relationships, Loud Women need to raise their standards. Whether you have been married twenty years or just starting a new romance, my hope is you will be in a relationship that makes you feel loved, worthy, and happy. Sadly, many women are not in these types of relationships. Many women are miserable inside—and sometimes outside too.

One reason for this misery is because women are innate givers and horrible receivers. Our lover might try to give back to us, and we reject it because we do not feel worthy. When you refuse to ask for help with a household chore because you do not want to bother your spouse, that's you not being a good receiver. That's you having low self-worth. If you are in a relationship where your partner is not giving you anything, even if you ask, you are not being a good receiver either because you are settling for not receiving *anything*. Again, this comes from low self-worth.

If you are like me, you feel like you want to receive but are too tired to ask for what you want. All that giving exhausts you. This can be compounded when your partner is not reciprocal in your relationship. It feels easier to do something yourself, or to keep your mouth shut and get over it.

These choices, though, are false ones. We have lots of choices when it comes to our romantic relationships. We just have to be brave enough to see them and choose. However, when low self-worth is propelling your side of the relationship, and your giving cup is empty, your choices feel limited.

Here's what I have started to ask myself: *Don't I deserve...?* For example, don't I deserve help around the house? Don't I deserve to be remembered for my birthday? Don't I deserve some cuddle time that does not lead to sex?

Yes, yes, and yes.

The beauty of asking this question is that it activates my Inner Loud Woman. Her voice pipes up, drowning out my Ego's, and confirms what I already know: *Yes, I am deserving.*

This same question works for friendships, too. Just like your romantic relationships, your friendships should make you feel loved, worthy, and happy. You would think this would be easier to attain because you do not have intimacy complicating matters. Not so much. Many women are in friendships that make them feel like shit. Women stay in these crappy friendships because they think this is what they deserve. And that's horse shit.

So, if you have a friend who borrows stuff (including money) without returning it, wants to compete with you on everything, or says mean things to you, it's time to ask yourself: *Don't I deserve...?* And the answer will always be yes.

And what if your lover or friend had a rough childhood or a bad first marriage? That is tragic in many ways, but it does not mean they can shit on you. What it does mean is that your lover or friend needs professional help to deal with this trauma. That way, they can fulfill their responsibility as a partner in your relationship.

Please do not let your friend or partner's past trauma be a crutch.

Of course, it is okay to sympathize and help them. What's not okay is to be their punching bag (literally or figuratively). Their trauma is not a permission slip to be a bad partner or friend.

Whoever wrote the rule that women must be selfless martyrs in their relationships was a misogynist. It does not help that culture supports this message. It was not that long ago when Tammy Wynette sang *Stand by Your Man*. Tammy, in a disastrous relationship, had low self-worth. Do not follow Tammy's lyrical advice. Instead, sing *Stand by My Self-Worth*. As you do, ignore the selfless martyr rule. Being a selfless martyr will not bring you happiness.

I am on this journey with you. I am listening to my Inner Loud Woman (who, thankfully, sounds more like Helen Reddy!) and demanding, *not asking*, for what I deserve out of all of my relationships. Am I doing this perfectly? No way. Do I sometimes revert to my old ways? Absolutely. Do I have to give myself pep talks? All the time.

Remember when I said you deserve relationships that make you feel loved, worthy, and happy? That's what I want for you; it's what I want for me, too. I may not know all the steps to get there, but I do know the first one: *It's recognizing we deserve healthy relationships.*

If you can wrap your arms around this fact, you are on your way. It does not matter how small it is—whether it's help folding laundry or having your own bucket of popcorn at the movies—you deserve it. You get to demand it. You get to have it.

I like to think our partners and friends will be happy to hear from us. They're fumbling along too. Sure, if you have a relationship with a guy (romantic or not), there are patriarchal issues to deal with, but at the core, I hope you have a relationship with a decent, imperfect human being who wants to love you better. Truthfully, he deserves to know how to be a better partner, right? So, tell him.

You can do this if you lift your self-worth. If you believe you are worthy of all the good things a healthy relationship brings, you have conquered a huge first step.

Loud Woman, please raise your self-worth. Your relationships count on it. Your happiness counts on it. Your heart counts on it, too.

And you deserve it, so much. I am saying this to myself as I say it to you. Let's lift our self-worth like a balloon to the sky. How beautiful would that be?

12

GUILT

My sons and husband played in the pool as I stood in front of my bathroom mirror, carefully applying eyeliner. I was going out for a desperately needed Girls' Night Out.

As I put the finishing touches on my eye make-up, I could hear my family splashing and laughing just outside my window. And then, a piercing cry from my three-year-old. I rushed outside to see what was going on. All I could see was blood.

My husband sat my son on the edge of the pool. I rushed over and saw a large, deep cut on the bottom of my son's chin. I ran back inside to get a towel to stop the bleeding.

My son had slipped as he tried to jump into the pool, and his chin caught the pool's edge. As we stopped the blood, it became apparent that my son needed stitches.

My mind raced as the options laid out before me. Did I continue with my Girls' Night Out plans, letting my more-than-capable husband handle the emergency room visit? Or, did I cancel my plans and head to the hospital with my three-year-old?

I knew if I went out with my sister and friends, I would not enjoy myself. The control enthusiast in me would demand every detail of my son's emergency room visit. In addition, I would be wracked with guilt. How could a mother leave her son who needed stitches? Would my son feel abandoned in his moment of need? How selfish could I be to enjoy an evening out while my son bled from his head?

It took just a few seconds to decide. Together, we took my son to the emergency room. He was a trooper, handling the scary hospital without batting an eye and endured the gluing up of his chin. When we got home, I headed to the bathroom to wash off my make-up with new nagging thoughts racing through my head.

If I had not planned a Girls' Night Out, would my son had gotten injured? If I had planned to stay home, as I did every Saturday night, could this whole incident have been avoided? In essence, I was blaming myself for my son's injury.

This is what happens when you don't have enough self-worth to enjoy self-care. This is what happens when you feel unworthy of taking care of yourself or putting your needs first.

I could fill pages with similar stories, especially once I became a mom. I believed my kids' needs *always* came before my own, to the point of sacrificing not just fun times—but my physical and mental health. I was a ticking time bomb that finally started to go off one day at work.

I sat in my office, chatting with my co-worker, when suddenly, I felt like I was going to pass out. Panic filled my body. A nurse colleague took my blood pressure and checked my pulse—all high—and encouraged me to call my doctor. My physician saw me later that day and found nothing wrong with me physically.

A few days later, I felt like a stone was lodged in my chest. Did I head to the ER? No, I went to my computer and paid the bills. Why? Because I didn't want my husband to worry about figuring out what bills needed to be paid in case he rushed me to the hospital. After paying the bills, I stretched out on the couch and woke up feeling better. Crisis averted.

But I was not well at all. The stone-in-the-chest feeling came back when I was at work—to the point where my co-worker took me to the emergency room. I had a kind, smart emergency room physician who ran a battery of tests and confirmed that my heart was very healthy.

The pain in my chest was from costochondritis, which is when your rib cage cartilage gets inflamed. He also said that my other symptoms, such as shortness of breath, resulted from anxiety.

You would think this would have assured me, but my emergency room visit sent me down a more frightening path. Again, my physical and mental health had endured years of coming in last, and it was not done getting my attention. My anxiety got worse. I lost a lot of weight in a short period of time and battled shortness of breath. My coping mechanisms were shot, constantly crying and staying in a state of absolute fear.

My primary care doctor suggested I see a therapist while she worked on finding me the right anti-anxiety medicine. It took months for me to feel "normal" again. During this time, I discovered mindfulness practices and guided meditations. I would ask my husband to watch the boys while I laid on our bed, breathing in rhythm to the soft voices coming from my iPod. Eventually, I began to feel better, but here's what had to happen first:

I had to stop putting my needs last. My body sent that message loud and clear. The chest pain, shortness of breath, spacey feeling in my head—these were all signals that I was not taking care of myself. After years of putting everyone else's needs before my own, it was time to shift priorities.

It was hard as hell. But it was necessary because I knew my next emergency room visit would be for something more serious unless I took care of my needs now.

Have you ever heard of the expression "you can't pour from an empty cup?" Your cup empties every time you take care of someone else. It's okay to be nurturing and caring, but you cannot keep it up unless you refill your cup with unapologetic, guilt-free self-care.

For me, I had to unravel a lot to get to the point where I could refill my cup. I had to wrap my head around this realization: *I was worthy of putting myself first* (I resisted this realization at first). I started my self-worth practice by taking time for myself—from naps to walks around the block. That trickled into meditation and journaling. I began reading personal development books, too. As I worked on my self-worth, I could feel my body feeling better. It's almost as if my body heaved a big sigh of relief with each nap, walk, and meditation. I remain on the journey, of course, but when I look back at how far I've come, I am proud of myself. When I increased my self-worth and reprioritized my needs, my body felt better.

In addition, you have to make time for your self-care and draw boundaries around this time. For a giver like me, this was hard. It meant I had to ask for help. As a mom with two young sons, I wanted to think I could do all and be all. Asking for help felt like I was shattering my "I have it together" image. Plus, it felt like I was letting my kids down somehow.

These are the guilt messages perpetuated by societal conditioning, and none of them are true. Asking for help is a sign of strength and high self-worth. My first requests for help were shaky and imperfect, but as I asked for more help, I gained more confidence. I saw that it was okay.

You too are worthy of guilt-free self-care. Please do not push your needs to the bottom of the list for so long that your body freaks out. I do not wish panic attacks on anyone, and if you can avoid panic attacks by taking care of yourself now, do it.

Here's the thing: By believing I am worthy of taking care of myself, I relished my self-care times and it made me a happier person. I was more patient with the kids. I was more confident about my work. I smiled more. It was a lovely ripple effect!

You deserve this too. All Loud Women do, and it's time we allow our cups to be refilled—without explanation, apology, or guilt.

13

INSTAGRAM PERFECTION

I had just finished a two-mile walk when a good idea dropped into my brain: *I should shoot a video about working through distracting times.* My brain quickly filled with tips—all good ones—and I didn't want to lose my thought.

What was stopping me, though, was my appearance. No make-up, hair in a messy ponytail, workout clothes—I did not feel "camera ready."

I deliberated: Do I shoot this video now while I feel inspired, or do I go in and perfect my appearance?

I made the video. As I watched the recording, I honed in on the bags under my eyes and my blotchy skin. I felt ugly and "less than," but I hoped my Instagram followers heard my message nonetheless.

Guess what? They did. That video is one of my most popular ones. And to think I almost didn't shoot it because of my appearance!

Have you ever seen women's Instagram photos that look so damn perfect? Perfect hair, perfect living room, perfect kids, perfect cookies, perfect bookshelf.

(And then compare this to guys' photos: baseball caps covering imperfect hair, five o'clock shadows, disheveled desks, and stains on T-shirts. More on that later...)

Instagram Perfection is a thing. It's when women only show the shining highlights of their lives: The best picture of themselves, the best backgrounds behind their desks, the best outfits on their kids, and the best tablescapes in their dining rooms.

Everything is shiny, clean, coifed, and curled.

As you scroll through these snapshots of Instagram perfection, you may start to feel less than perfect. You glance around your house, and see piles of dirty clothes and cat hair amassed on the carpet. Your hair is in some kind of weird bun, and you're not sure if you brushed your teeth today. Lunch was a bowl of cereal that is still sitting at the corner of your desk.

Yet, if you were to take a photo for Instagram, you probably would style your hair, brush your teeth, change your shirt, and clean up the cat hair, right?

Why?

Because we are obsessed with the illusion of perfection, and that's especially true when it comes to sharing photos and stories on social media.

This is undesirable for two reasons:

1. You're only posting the good stuff, and life is made up of bad and good things.
2. You start to compare your life to those Instagram perfect posts.

This results in a shitty mindset, bad self-image, and low self-worth.

While we can't control what other people post on their social media accounts, we can control what we post. What if we showed the front and back of our lives?

The front may be your honor roll son who scored the winning touchdown at Friday night's game. The back is how much anxiety your son has about getting into the college of his choice or being broken-hearted by a girl who dumped him for another guy.

The front may be your gorgeous beach-waved hair and fake

eyelashes, posing by a perfectly plumped Pottery Barn pillow. The back may be the big zit on your chin that you expertly covered and the squabble with your husband before that photo shoot.

You see? Everything has a front and back, and if you ask me, it's the back that shows our humanity. It's the back that brings connection. It's the back that spawns conversations (and isn't that what social media is really about?).

I want to challenge you, Loud Woman, to post more than the highlights of your life. Yes, brag about your kids or show off your fancy photo. But show us imperfect pictures, too. Not only will feel better (once you express your vulnerability, it's like a boulder has been lifted from your shoulders), you will make others feel better too. We have more in common, than not, and your "back" stories may help someone feel a little less alone in her journey.

Now let's talk about how we perceive those perfect photos on Instagram. Admire them, sure, but don't think any less of yourself. If you start to feel like shit, remember what I said: *Everything has a front and back, and you are just seeing the front:*

- You are seeing one photo out of dozens of discarded ones.
- You are seeing someone after hours in hair and make-up.
- You are seeing a living room after an extensive cleaning with a staging expert on hand.

You are not seeing the back:

- How she bribed her honor-roll, touchdown-making son to study for the test he "aced."
- How she is self-conscious of the little space between her front teeth.
- How she is taking pills and chugging coffee to get through the day.

While writing this book, I began waking up at 4 a.m. I'm not sure why: hormones, anxiety, household noises—who knows! One morning, I decided to post about my plight on social media. I wrote vulnerably about reaching a certain age where early mornings would be the norm and how I was making peace with it. I talked about what I accomplished that morning and how my pets were happy to see me. I took a selfie with no make-up covering the morning bags under my eyes or acne scars, disheveled hair, and stained T-shirt. Guess what? It spawned amazing social media conversations. Why? Because other "women of a certain age" were going through the same thing. They could relate. They laughed and commiserated. Our "certain age" insomnia united us.

My intention for this section is to give you permission to be yourself on social media. I am not suggesting you don't post your professional headshots or brag about your son's achievements. Our world needs good news, and your triumphs are worthy of sharing.

What I am asking, though, is twofold. First, be more vulnerable on social media. Second, remember that when you see Instagram perfection you are really seeing a staged glimpse of someone's imperfect life.

What if we, as women, take a page from a guy's social media handbook and just appear in our baseball caps with a messy bed behind us? Would the world fall apart? No. Would people think less of you? Probably not (and if they do, they are not your people). Would you feel better? More than likely.

Which leads me to this: *Social media can be a validation rabbit hole.* From collecting followers to seeking people's approval on what you post, many women use social media to validate themselves and their ideas.

Let's say you posted a picture of yourself on Instagram because you want people to say you like nice, or pretty, or gorgeous. And then you wait, hoping your photo finds its way to your followers' news feeds. At first, no one is commenting, and your heart drops. Then the comments start to come in, and you read each one multiple times, savoring them. You feel validated. You feel beautiful.

This scenario I just wrote? That's my story.

It's an obsession—the waiting for the comments, the sad feeling when they aren't coming in right away, followed by the elation when they do.

If this scenario resonates with you, you are not alone. You and I are seeking validation through social media, and it's killing our mindset. The good news is we can change this.

The need for social media validation derives from low self-worth. Simply put, we use other people's opinions to fill our self-worth, instead of finding self-worth from within. Loud Woman, we need to step away from this feeling because it's making us powerless.

Here's where the need for social media validation gets dangerous for women: When we require social media validation before making a decision or to proceed with our lives in some way. When we crowd-source decisions, or ask people to validate the decision we have made, we are putting our lives in the hands of strangers.

It's time to be confident about what we say and in our decisions. We must trust our intelligence. No longer should we turn to social media and cyberspace strangers to validate what we are saying, or how we look, or the decisions we make. We must stop relying on other people's feedback to steer our boats.

And if you are seeking validation through collecting fans and followers, this is unhealthy too. Fans and followers are not postage stamps. A stamp collector will tell you to not just collect *any* stamp—just the ones of value.

Unfortunately, social media has become a land of *quantity desire*—the most fans, likes, comments, and shares. What does a great quantity of any of these things mean? Well, it could mean you paid for advertising to get your stuff out there. It could also mean you beat the algorithm somehow. Either way, it's a vicious cycle, and when you seek validation through social media, you are caught in it.

Your value as a person has nothing to do with social media quantities, and your value also has nothing to do with what other people think. When you get on the other side of this need for validation, you will feel so much better. I know because I am on this journey, too.

FEMINISM

I will not have my life narrowed down. I will not bow down to somebody else's whim or to someone else's ignorance.

— BELL HOOKS

14

REGRET

Tears puddled around the edges of my eyes as I watched the news. Around the world, from Washington, D.C. to London, millions of women, children, and men marched to proclaim: *Women's rights are civil rights.* It was a beautiful sight. Their signs made me laugh, the speeches gave me hope, and the pink wave of pussy hats filled my heart with feminist pride.

I cried out of gratitude. I cried out of love. And I cried out of regret. Why regret? Because I chose not to participate in the 2017 Women's March.

I have been told your biggest regrets are the things you don't do. Time and time again, when I don't do something, I always regret it. As I watched those pink pussy hats and empowered marchers, regret flooded me like a river coursing through a canyon.

I am a feminist. Usually, I never shy away from this title, despite being bashed for it. Many times in the past, men and women have called me a "feminazi" or "man-hater."

When Donald Trump won the presidential election in 2016, I worried his administration would reverse the positive steps taken by women, members of the LGBQ+ community, people of color, immigrants, and followers of different faiths.

As long as I have been aware of Donald Trump, I associated him with exploiting money and women. It seemed he felt entitled to both, at any cost.

The leaked "hot mic" tape from 2005 showcased exactly how Donald Trump feels about women, when he said, among other things: "Grab 'em by the pussy. You can do anything." [15]

When I heard the tape and read the transcript, I wanted to punch a wall. I was not surprised, though, by his words. Look at his marriages, past sexual assault accusations, and how he treats his oldest daughter. His feelings about women were always out in the open. Now we knew what Trump said *privately* about women.

I believed that tape would nail Trump's political coffin closed. Men and women of any political persuasion could see Trump was sexist and blatantly disrespectful toward women.

Wow, was I wrong. I woke up the morning of November 9, 2016, to discover Donald Trump won the election. Our country elected a known sexist (among other things) to the White House. I wanted to throw up and cry. I could not wrap my arms around this thought: *How could a man who said such denigrating things about women now be our leader?*

More questions plagued my mind: What would happen to legal abortions? Access to birth control? Protections in the workplace? Equal pay?

Then I thought about the rights of women of color, LGBQ+ women, women who have been sexually assaulted, women who suffer from domestic violence - the list went on and on. As it did, I could feel my heart getting heavier, as if it was sliding down my rib cage.

You would think, with all of these swirling thoughts, that I would be the perfect candidate for the Women's March, right?

No.

Don't get me wrong: I wanted this movement to spread worldwide. People recognized that we have much more work to do. Logistically, I could have participated in a Women's March because one was organized in the Tampa Bay area, near where I live.

I had every reason to march, but it only took one thing to stop me: Fear.

No, not fear of getting hurt or arrested.

My fear centered on what my local friends would think.

All of my local friends—the folks I saw at my son's football game and in the candy aisle at Target—are die-hard Trump fans. In a sea of red, I am a lone blue speck.

While I could not (and would never) support Donald Trump, I remained committed to *not* judge my friends for their presidential choice (I did judge them if they voted for him 2020, though.) They have a right to vote for whoever they like, whether I like their choice or not. I believed our friendship was bigger than political ideologies.

While I believed this, I also saw what was going on around me. The 2016 election brought out so much hate and vitriol from both sides. Conservatives called Democrats "snowflakes" or "libtards," and accused Democrats of being "butt hurt" about losing the election. Liberals called Republicans sexists and racists, and accused them of supporting a man who cheated his way to the presidency.

As the division widened, conservatives and liberals alike got bolder with their language. Social media discussions were shit shows. TV shows were yelling matches. People were "going-for-the-jugular" confrontational.

Confrontation scared me the most. I knew families were not speaking to each other because of political confrontations. The same with friends. And I had to ask: Was Donald Trump worth this division —not only in our nation but in our dining rooms?

I did not want a confrontation with my friends. So, I stayed home and hid. I sat behind my computer screen and watched the videos pour in from around the world.

While my Facebook news feed filled with empowering messages from the Women's March, another theme popped up: The disdain for the Women's March by my female conservative friends.

One friend said she was at the beach, basking in the rights she enjoyed as an American.

Another posted a meme about how she was one of millions of women who marched to the polls to vote for Donald Trump.

Yet another friend posted about how tired she was of "vagina hats," and how these women should be ashamed of themselves because American women have it so much better than women in other countries.

(Side note: Yes, I am grateful for not being flogged in public. Or for not being forced to wear certain clothes. And for having a driver's license. This does not mean I can't want the same things American men receive, such as equal pay. I'll talk about that later.)

Reading their messages filled with me with two emotions. I felt rage because these privileged women were so oblivious about what was going on around them.

Secondly, and strangely, I felt validated about staying home. What would these friends think if they learned I had marched?

My validation waned quickly. It then turned to anger.

Holy shit, I am a feminist! I've been combatting people's opinions about my feminism for years. Shouldn't a feminist attend a Women's March in spite of what others think?

Yes, she should. As I pondered this, my anger subsided, and regret moved in. I was not being my true self. Instead of participating in something I believed in, I cowered behind my computer and watched from the sidelines—all because I was swayed by a narrative created in my head.

Thankfully, regrets beget lessons. And my decision to not attend the 2017 Women's March taught me a lot. I was reminded, once again, that I regret the things I do not do. I learned to stop hiding from the causes that are important to me. I also was reminded to express my opinion unapologetically and to stop worrying about what other people think.

Finally, I learned this: There is nothing wrong with being a feminist. It's a badge I wear with honor. I will never shrink from it again.

We have lots of work to do. This work will *not* get done unless feminists, like me, stop hiding. This work *will get done* if feminists, like me, get out there and pressure our government officials, corporations, clergy, and other influencers to change laws, policies, and mindsets about women's rights. It is time to get Louder so we can get this work done.

15

I AM WOMAN

We climbed into my parents' Honda Civic, and Mom pushed an 8-track into the car stereo. Helen Reddy blared from our little speakers, exclaiming *I Am Woman*.

I was too young to understand the meaning of the song's words, but I could pick up on the empowerment of each lyric. I hummed along, imagining a strong woman—one who looked just like Mom—roaring like a lion.

This was my first taste of feminism.

Later, when I was in third grade, my music teacher Mr. Henry Fletcher played *I Am Woman* on his electronic piano. As his fingers stroked the keys, Mr. Fletcher explained how women around the world sang this song to feel strong and powerful. He pointed out that the "brother" referenced in the song represented those men who didn't quite buy into women's strength and power.

Oh, I know how that feels, I thought.

I had already witnessed how the boys in my class didn't think girls were strong. The boys said girls couldn't be the captain of the kickball team. Or they insisted I couldn't outrun any of them.

My eight-year-old body was fast and capable and strong. I could do the things these boys said I couldn't, but because they were boys, they got their way.

As I tossed these scenarios around in my young brain, I began to more fully understand what Helen sang about.

I fully blossomed into a feminist in the tenth grade, thanks to my English teacher, Ms. Wanda Detlefsen. I love how she preferred "Ms." as her title, even as a married woman and mother (she was married to Mr. Detlefsen, who taught American History at the school, too).

Ms. D showed us how some literature upheld traditional gender roles, holding up kids' books with moms dressed in aprons and dads hurrying off to work. We read *The Scarlet Letter*, and she never once denigrated Hester Prynne for her choices, but Ms. D gave us an earful about Arthur Dimmesdale and Roger Chillingworth. I never read a fiction book the same way again.

As I emerged from Ms. D's class as a sixteen-year-old, I proclaimed myself a feminist. As I look back at my teenage years, I smile in the knowledge that, despite my many mistakes, I got *that* part right.

In this section, let's take a closer look at feminism. We'll examine what feminism really is (and is not) and specify reasons why some women choose not to be called a feminist. Finally, we'll take a look at intersectional feminism, a term you probably have heard but may not understand.

I am woman. I am a feminist. Are you? Turn the page to learn more.

16

WHAT IS FEMINISM, REALLY?

I once read a social media comment written by a seventeen-year-old young woman who declared she is not a feminist.

Her reason? Quite simply, she loves men. She has a great dad, supportive brothers, and a loving boyfriend. She could not label herself a feminist because she believed feminism to be a man-hating ideology.

This was not the first time I had heard women say they do not align with feminism. Their reasons vary, but one thing seems to be a common thread: Feminism almost feels like a dirty word—something you whisper or even denounce.

This makes me sad. That's why it's time to address the elephant in the room—and that is feminism. I cannot write a book about becoming a Loud Woman without tackling what feminism is (and isn't).

My hope is twofold: If you already identify as a feminist, your belief will be affirmed, and you will understand why other women have turned their backs against feminism. Second, if identifying as a feminist makes you uncomfortable, you will learn why that's the case and hopefully become more comfortable with this title.

So, let's start with this declaration: You're likely a feminist, even if you don't believe you are.

How do you feel when you read this sentence?

If it makes you uneasy, that's okay. Feminism has been put through the wringer in recent years, and you may not feel aligned to it.

Who would want to align with a movement that's been defined as the following?

- "[I]n the past few decades, this idea of women's rights has evolved to mean some sort of additional, special rights or privileges that position us above men, categorically. Though feminists won't admit it, this isn't actually equality. It's playing governmental favoritism and demanding to in fact not be equal. Feminism has gone from demanding equality to demanding entitlements."[16] **Dr. Jenna Ellis**, assistant professor of Legal Studies and Leadership at Colorado Christian University

- "Feminists are imprisoned by their negative view of women and their place in the world around them.... Feminists believe marriage and motherhood are oppressive.... Feminists believe there are no differences between males and females other than their sex organs (and now even those can be changed!)."[17] **Suzanne Zecker**, author

- "The whole point of modern-era feminazi-ism is embodied in my undeniable truth of life number 24: Feminism was established so as to allow unattractive women easier access to the mainstream of pop culture."[18] **Rush Limbaugh**, radio host

No wonder people do not want to be known as feminists! If you believe these definitions, feminists are ugly women who hate men and motherhood, and want government entitlements. If I followed this definition, I would not want to be called a feminist either.

Here's the thing: Feminism is none of these things. Feminism, according to *Merriam-Webster*, is "the theory of political, economic, and social equality of the sexes."

And now let's look at how some women define feminism:

- "My own definition of a feminist is a man or a woman who says, 'Yes, there's a problem with gender as it is today and we must fix it, we must do better.' *All* of us, women and men, must do better."[19] **Chimamanda Ngozi Adichie**
- "Believing that people should make their own choices about their own lives is ultimately what I think it means to be a feminist...For me, being a feminist means believing that women, and everyone, really, have the right to live life on their own terms, and that is why I define myself as such. When we strip it down to its bare definition, everyone should be a feminist."[20] **Luvvie Ajayi Jones**
- "I look at myself as a product of my choices, not a victim of circumstances, and that's really to me what conservative feminism, if you will, is all about."[21] **Kellyanne Conway**
- "A feminist is anyone who recognizes the equality and full humanity of women and men."[22] **Gloria Steinem**

As I read these personal definitions, plus the dictionary one, two themes emerge:

1. Equality between the sexes
2. Freedom to choose

Notice what is not listed here:

1. Women are better than men
2. Hating men
3. Hating marriage
4. Not wanting to be a mother
5. Telling you what to do with your body
6. Telling you who you can love (or not love)

I define feminism as a movement that advocates for women to have the same rights as men, and the freedom for women to choose how to live their lives.

Feminism is not about "better." It is about equality. Yet many people resist the movement. Why? Because feminism scares them. Here are some common reasons:

- Fear of upsetting men (when men get upset, women go into "coddle" mode, meaning we will not identify as a feminist to make men happy)
- Fear of losing security and protection
- Fear of abandonment
- Fear of being disliked
- Fear of what others may think
- Fear of losing financial control
- Fear of losing power

Whatever it is, when fear drives your reasoning, you can bet the reasoning is wrong. Fear is a lens that clouds better judgement.

Yet, if you ask people what they think feminism is, some will respond with comments about men, marriage, childbearing, household structure, and more.

You see: Feminism has nothing to do with any of those things. When you hear that it does, ignore the message.

Instead, remember what feminism is *really* about: equal rights for women and women's freedom to choose how to live their lives.

That's it. Nothing more.

Let's not forget that many of the freedoms and liberties American women now enjoy are recent developments. We now have rights that women did not have even fifty to a hundred years ago: the right to vote, the ability to get your own credit card, protections around sexual harassment in the workplace and pregnancy discrimination, and the ability to marry who you want.

How did we get these rights? From the work of feminists who fought tirelessly for equality and freedom. Yes, we still have lots of work to do. Pay inequality, sexual assault victims' rights, sexism in sports, domestic violence, and the continued discrimination of black, brown, and LGBTQ+ women still plague us. And it will not get fixed until men and women begin to identify themselves as feminists and work together to makes these changes.

Please do not turn the page until you can wrap your arms around what feminism *really* is: equality between the sexes and freedom to choose. These are big goals, for sure, but ones that can be achieved when you and every other Loud Woman out there declare themselves *feminists*.

17

NON-FEMINISTS

When the #MeToo movement took off, one of my dear friends, who had considered herself a feminist, began to feel disenfranchised with the feminist movement.

She watched as story after story about power-hungry, sexist men came to light, and then watched with equal horror as people began calling *all men* power-hungry and sexist.

My friend is married to a wonderful guy, and together, they are raising two conscientious boys. While she could agree that some men are evil, she could not, and would not, go down any path that generalized all men that way.

That's when she decided to stop calling herself a feminist.

Do you feel the same way? If you do not yet consider yourself a feminist, I want to pause for a moment and honor your stance. This is how you feel, and you are worthy of being your true self.

This gives us an important opportunity to delve into why some Loud Women are not on board with feminism. While the reasons are personal, I think we can find similar themes. Here are some reasons I have discovered why some women do not align with feminism:

- They attribute feminism to man hating, and they love men.

- They find feminism to be anti-marriage and anti-mothering, which do not align with their beliefs.
- These women believe in a more traditional, often-religious definition of marriage and relationships, and they believe feminism violates these beliefs.
- They believe we have already achieved equal rights and think the feminist movement is no longer needed and that we should be grateful for the rights we already have.
- They are comfortable with the status quo and do not want to change it.
- These women believe in equal rights and agree there is work to be done, but the feminist movement feels out of alignment with their beliefs around politics and reproductive health.

This list of reasons is not comprehensive. However, these overarching themes provide a glimpse into the rationale of why some women do not embrace feminism.

On your Loud Woman journey, you will find women who are not feminists. I encourage you to learn more from them. Ask questions and listen. Do not try to change their minds because I believe, at the core of it, all Loud Women are feminists. They just have different ideas on what feminism is (or is not).

If you put these Loud Women on the defensive by trying to change their minds, it will backfire. Instead, let us honor their position and weed through the rhetoric to get to the core of their issues with feminism.

Think about how you talk about feminism. Are you assuring men and women that it is not about man hating? Are you advocating for women to have choices with their reproductive health, including the idea that they, as individuals, are anti-abortion? Are you respectful of the choices a woman is making as a wife, even if you disagree with it?

At the end of the day, feminism is about choice. If a woman chooses to have a traditional marriage, or is anti-abortion, or is happy with the rights she already has, it is her choice, and we must respect it. We do not have to agree, but we must respect her choices.

Feminism has room for everyone. Just like how religions have different sects, feminism has many flavors too. Some may embrace a more conservative view of feminism, while others may take a more liberal approach. They are opposites, but neither are wrong.

Why do some women think they are not feminists? Because they believe the wrong definition of feminism. As Loud Women, we must work harder to teach that feminism is a spectrum. That way, those who identify as non-feminists can see they are feminists. Until this happens, we will continue to fight amongst ourselves, which will hinder everyone's Loud Woman journey.

18

INTERSECTIONAL FEMINISM

I wish I had paid greater attention to the black women with whom I went to college.

I attended a small women's college where most of the students were white. In fact, black women had only been attending my alma mater for about twenty years before my arrival in 1990. By the time I attended, most of the student body still were young white women. I don't think even ten percent of our students were of color.

Black women who did attend Wesleyan College usually joined the Black Student Alliance (BSA). In my naïveté (and racism, I'm embarrassed to admit), I thought these students joined BSA to talk about their common heritage. Little did I know (or want to understand), these BSA members were talking about the racist treatment they received from the college, faculty, and fellow students. They talked about how the road to equality was so different, harder, than their fellow white students. They advocated for a larger voice on campus, in the community, and in the world.

Sure, I believed that black women were my equal, but I did not understand that my activism as a feminist was not benefiting them. I also didn't realize feminism for me, as a white woman, was different than for my black classmates. These black women told me, of course, but I was not listening. I was missing intersectional feminism, as I would later learn, from my advocacy.

What is intersectional feminism? American Law Professor Kimberle' Crenshaw coined the term intersectional feminism in 1989, describing it as "a prism for seeing the way in which various forms of inequality often operate together and exacerbate each other."[23]

Think of equality as a road map. One street is the equality a person seeks as a black citizen. Another street is the equality this same person seeks as a woman. And a third street is the equality she seeks as a lesbian. As these three roads intersect, they show the combination of these unique oppression experiences.

This is a simplistic example, of course. The prejudices women feel on any of these roads is different, even within the same race, or sexual orientation, or any other demographic. For example, a black woman in her fifties probably has different experiences than a black woman thirty years younger.

Nevertheless, what remains true for all women is this: Traditional advocacy only looks at one street. Intersectional feminism requires us to look at *all* streets, and how they intersect, as a part of the entire experience of oppression and discrimination.

Intersectional feminism reminds us to *not* just look at the unequal treatment of women; it requires us to look at the spectrum of oppression experienced by women of different races, religions, socioeconomic levels, sexual orientation, and more.

The traditional feminism movement has made great strides for women, but middle-to-upper class, heterosexual white women have been the biggest benefactors so far. Traditionally, for any improvement to occur for women, it must first get the attention of these wealthier white women.

That's why it is essential for white women to be an intersectional feminist. If a woman of color tells you something is unjust or unequal, we must believe her and advocate for justice. It also means we must check our privilege.

At the early stages of the coronavirus pandemic, I saw a Facebook post where a woman pled for people to wear masks, asking them to envision a new mother going to the store to buy diapers. What if this new mom got sick? What if the newborn got COVID-19? How terrifying it would be for that family—and potentially deadly.

This scenario prompted another woman to respond, recommending that the new mom get a service to deliver the diapers from the store or have her spouse go to the store instead. Now, these suggestions are not terrible, but it's an example of privilege. She assumed the new mom could afford the delivery service. She also assumed the new mom was married.

For many women, paying for a delivery service is out of the question. They cannot afford it. Furthermore, many women are single moms with no support system. To assume this new mom can call someone for help is tone deaf.

What was a seemingly innocent response shows you how privilege skews our vision about how the world works.

That's where intersectional feminism comes in. By being intersectional in our pursuit for equality, we are ensuring *every* woman is included. Any other form of feminism leads to the oppression of others.

We will explore later in this book how White Loud Women can support women of color, but for now, let's remember this:

The Loud Woman Journey will be different for each woman. Yes, some of these differences will stem from different mindsets. However, the greatest differences will result from our different races, ages, abilities, geographic locations, socioeconomic status, sexual orientation, and more. Let's work together to ensure each Loud Woman's journey is recognized—and that no Loud Woman is left behind.

BOUNDARIES

You have to be able to set boundaries, otherwise the rest of the world is telling you who you are and what you should be doing. You can still be a nice person and set boundaries.

— OPRAH WINFREY

19

BOUNDARY QUEEN

I am an early riser. I blame it on my pets, but the truth is I love getting up before everyone else in the morning. I teeter to the kitchen with my phone and water bottle in hand, and proceed with my morning routine—feeding the pets, emptying the dishwasher, and preparing my breakfast.

It was a September morning, like any other, as I finished up my morning tasks and headed to my computer. As I laid my phone down, I noticed something unusual: I missed a call from an hour before. The voice mail time stamp said 5:11 a.m., and I could tell it was a long voice mail.

Oh shit. Something happened to Mom.

My mother lives in an assisted living facility, and she has fallen many times in the middle of the night. It would not be the first time that her facility called about a fall.

I quickly hit the play button, and a woman's clipped voice greeted me with this message:

 I don't know who you are, or how you're getting my email address, but you're some kind of fraud. I've never visited your website. I have no idea who the fuck you are, and you're spamming, so I'm going to take this to the fullest extent of the law. I would never visit this marketing site ever, ever. Never even signed up for shit yet you have my personal email address. Then when you go to unsubscribe, it keeps bringing you back, and I keep getting your emails. I don't know who you are Jill Celeste; you're not my friend, and if you think this is spiritual, you are jamming yourself with karma. You better watch yourself on soliciting private emails, you fucking piece of garbage. I have never been interested in marketing. I have never clicked a fucking ad of yours, so how have you gotten my private address? I'm having you investigated. Do not solicit my phone number at all. I will prosecute you, whoever you are, whatever you are. How fucking dare you!

The hairs on the back of my neck stood straight up, and my heart pounded. I had no idea who this woman was, and I couldn't believe she was this mad to leave a 5 a.m. voice mail about an email she received from me.

I listened to her message again. Her voice dripped with vitriol. Her tone and message scared the shit out of me, not just because of her threatened legal action, but because she was so pissed about getting an email from me that she grabbed her phone and called me at five in the morning. Truthfully, I worried she was a little unhinged.

I checked my customer management software, and sure enough, this woman had opted into my list when she requested a free copy of my book. I could see when and where she opted in, and that she opened the confirmation email and downloaded the PDF of my book. I could also see she had opened a subsequent email.

Assured I had not done anything wrong, I emailed her back. I shared screen shots of our email relationship. At the end of the email, I typed, "Do not contact me again, ever." After I sent the email, I removed her from my email list, and blocked her email address from my server and her cell number from my phone.

Then, I took a long look at my customer communication process. You see: When you send a marketing email, you must include a phone number and address on every communication. Naively, I had included my cell number and home address.

A few hours later, I secured a post office box and a Google phone number, which replaced my personal information on my emails. I felt safer, for sure, but I was not done.

As a marketing mentor, I wanted to be available to my clients. Therefore, they could reach me by phone, text, email, and Facebook direct messaging. The contact page on my website listed multiple ways to reach me.

The truth is that if you don't set up boundaries, you will get stepped on. I got stepped on by this pissed-off lady, and it was scary. I did not ever want to go through it again.

That morning, I learned I needed firmer boundaries all around me. I protected my cell phone number and home address. I have a super-secret email that only a handful of people know. I turned off my Facebook Messenger, which discourages people from messaging me.

Someone once coined me the "Boundary Queen." It's a title I am proud of, but it's one I earned from making a lot of mistakes.

Thanks to my boundaries, if a pissed-off lady wants to reach me at 5 a.m., she won't, at least not on a personal device. She'll be greeted with kind, automated systems and dealt with swiftly but firmly. I do not deserve an f-bomb-filled 5 a.m. voice mail. I do not deserve to be threatened with a lawsuit for not doing anything wrong. I do not deserve to feel scared. Some folks may not agree, and that's where boundaries come in. My boundaries are my force field that surround me, protecting my mindset, dignity, and self-worth, bouncing f-bombs and hostile people back into the ether—away from me, my family, and my heart.

20

YOUR NEEDS GO FIRST

B oundaries are those spaces you create around you to protect your mindset, energy levels, health, relationships, cash flow, and other aspects of your life that are precious to you.

Women often have difficulty creating boundaries because we have been conditioned to think about everyone else's needs first.

As a Loud Woman, it's time to abandon this "my needs are last" mindset because it's not serving you.

Why should your needs come after everyone else's all the time? They shouldn't, and that is why it's time to focus on creating boundaries in your life.

As you think about establishing boundaries, you will probably hear the word "selfish" pop up in your head. It's a shame selfish is considered a bad word. Perhaps people are confusing selfish with stingy. Being stingy is not what we want. Stingy comes from a place of scarcity, and the world is abundant.

Selfish is about believing your needs matter, and because the world will encroach on your needs, you must create boundaries to protect yourself and your needs.

Picture a map. Countries have boundaries, right? Someone created those boundaries to identify the country's geographical edges. Boundaries are clear. Boundaries prevent conflict. Boundaries are essential.

Imagine you are a country. Wouldn't you want to surround yourself with a boundary to ensure you are safe, happy, and balanced? I bet you would.

In this section, we will talk more about boundaries, including why you might have a hard time establishing them, different types of boundaries, and examples of how others have created boundaries.

At the end of this section, you will feel inspired to take a hard look at where you need to establish boundaries in your life.

One more thing before we delve in: Boundaries will piss people off. They always do. That's how you know they are working. You will set up boundaries despite pissy people—because the only happiness you can guarantee is your own.

UNRAVELING

E very Christmas, I relish watching *The Christmas Story*. I can recite most of the lines and laugh at the same scenes, despite seeing them dozens of times. While I love this story of Ralphie and his quest to get a Red Rider BB gun, there's one scene that strikes a little too close to home.

Ralphie's family gathers around the kitchen table, and as Mother sits down to eat her dinner, her family keeps asking her for something from the stove. Another slice of meat loaf. Another dollop of mashed potatoes. She gets up over and over again, while her meal—the one she just cooked—gets colder and colder.

"My mother had not had a hot meal for herself in 15 years," the narrator announced.

Whenever the movie gets to this scene, I want to shout, "Get your own food, Ralphie!" Not that my exclamation would matter. Mother will keep getting up because it's what she believes she's supposed to do, and Mother did not establish any boundaries to ensure she can sit down and eat the meal she just prepared.

Why do women have a hard time establishing boundaries? It's because we have been taught from an early age to be available, generous, self-sacrificing, and selfless. These all equate to a lack of boundaries.

Many of us watched our moms (and mother figures) give to their families, often sacrificing careers, hobbies, downtime—even the remote control—to make others happy. As we watched these women give, give, and give, we learned that's what women are supposed to do.

In other words, here is what society said to us:

Do you want to show your worth as a woman? Then, you must give selflessly, endlessly, and abundantly.

Years and years of watching the selfless giving by our grandmothers, mothers, stepmothers, aunts, neighborhood women, women on TV, women in movies, and women in commercials has taught us that we must do the same.

That's why, when you recognize that it's time for a boundary, you find it hard to do. You love your family, friends, clients, co-workers, and community. Won't they feel less loved by you if you create a boundary that stops, or at least restricts, your giving?

I saw this sentiment a lot when the coronavirus lockdowns happened. I can't count how many times I watched women entrepreneurs—both my friends and clients—give up their office space for their husbands and partners who had to start working from home. While these women were giving up their space, they were also giving up their time, helping their kids who were now learning from home.

This is a boundary issue. Why does the woman need to move her office? "Because he makes more money" is not the right answer. Why does the woman have to be the one assisting the kids with their virtual school work? "Because she has more flexibility with her calendar" is not the right answer either.

The right answer is because society has taught us that women must give selflessly, which means women are giving up their office space, time, income, and energy.

The remedy to this situation? Boundaries. Always boundaries!

Yet, so many women would be afraid to set up these boundaries because it's new and scary territory. Remember, we have been taught that to show our love and worth, we must give selflessly. How does creating a firm boundary around your office space or when you help your kids fit that narrative?

It doesn't fit. And that's why women did not set up these boundaries, and that's why women were tired and burned out during the pandemic, often quitting their jobs or businesses to juggle it all.

Here's the thing you need to remember: You can still love people *and* have boundaries. They go together, I promise.

Boundaries are a great expression of love because it shows those around you that you love yourself. That you cherish your mindset, health, time, and happiness. You show that self-love is as important as their love, and that by loving yourself enough to have boundaries, you create space in your life to love them so much more.

Creating boundaries is a great unraveling of everything you have been taught as a woman. Let's face it: It will be hard. You will have to undo the age-old expectation of selfless giving. You'll piss people off and have to work hard to not bend to their pressure.

But hard does not mean impossible or unnecessary. It also does not mean you shouldn't do it.

Don't be Mother from *The Christmas Story*. Unravel from the bullshit story that to selflessly give is the only way to show your love and worth. Put those boundaries up like a Star Trek force shield, even (and maybe especially) if it's hard to do so.

22

TYPES OF BOUNDARIES

Boundaries are the "guard rails" on our Loud Woman journey. You may be surprised where in your life you can create boundaries. Let's take a look at the different types of boundaries we can set up.

Physical: The physical space you take up in your home and workspace

- Who is allowed in your office, bedroom, etc.?
- Do you need to create a spot in your home that's just for you?
- Do you need alternate places outside of your home for work or hobbies?

Communication: How people can communicate with you

- How do you want your loved ones to reach out to you, especially during the work day?
- If you work from home, do you need to set up office hours so your family knows to not interrupt you?

- Have you turned off notifications on your phone? (More about that in the next chapter)

Time: How much time you are willing to allocate to things

- Do you need to set up time limits for personal matters during the work day?
- How much time do you want to spend with your family? Friends?
- How much time do you want to spend on social media? Watching Netflix?
- Do you need to allocate days of the week for specific tasks?
- Have you blocked off your holidays and vacation time?

Consumption: The news you will or will not consume, or spend time on

- How will you consume local, national, and international news (such as through social media, reading a newspaper, watching the evening news)?
- How much time will you spend consuming news?
- What news topics are off limits?
- What media outlets are your preferred sources for news?

Self-care: How you take care of yourself

- Do you need to set up specific times for self-care?
- How much sleep do you need daily?
- What foods and drinks are you consuming?
- How much exercise do you need weekly?
- Do you need to speak with your partner about your self-care?

Please do not try to implement all of these boundaries at once. This will be daunting and could set you up for failure. Instead, pick one type of boundary—maybe the one that will be the easiest to create —and implement from there. Gain confidence and then tackle the next category. However you approach it, please make sure you set up these boundaries. Loud Women put their needs first.

23

NOTIFICATIONS

The notifications on your phone are someone else's emergencies. We have trained ourselves to want to know the *instant* someone needs us by allowing notifications to rule our lives.

This is unhealthy. As a Loud Woman, it's time to value your time and boundaries, and that means you have permission to turn off your notifications, including those for social media.

I don't just say this: I practice this. If you looked at my phone right now, here's what you would discover:

- I have no notifications on for social media.
- I do not have email set up on my phone.
- My Facebook Messenger's Active Status is set to off.
- My phone is set to Do Not Disturb. My immediate family is listed as a "favorite," so if one of them tries to reach me, his call or text will come through.

What would I discover if I looked at your phone? I hope something similar.

You might be reading this, and thinking there is no way you could turn off your notifications, keep your phone on "do not disturb," or not have email on your phone. If this is you, I have a couple of questions to consider:

- Why do you have notifications on?
- What happens when you see a notification?

I will not pretend to know your answers to these questions—because we are grown-ass women with our own reasons—but I would like to share what answers came up for me. Perhaps my reasons will resonate with you.

WHY DO YOU HAVE NOTIFICATIONS ON?

I kept notifications on because I was afraid I was going to miss something, such as a call about my parents' health or my kid's behavior at school. I also wanted to know as soon as someone responded to my Facebook message or retweeted my blog post.

All seemed serious and important, and things I needed to know right away, no matter what I was doing. As an entrepreneur, this resulted in me being attached to my phone, even checking it while coaching my clients or writing marketing content.

I lived for that notification sound and pop-up message. Even if I tried to ignore them, I could not. I had to touch my phone.

Furthermore, I had convinced myself I was my family's only problem solver, nurturer, and chauffeur. If someone needed me, I could be reached right away, even at the risk of my privacy, work time, and family time.

I lived by my notifications and could never focus on any task, for fear or concern that I was missing something. It was draining.

Here's the thing: The only thing I was "missing" was living a life the way I wanted to live. That's when I decided to remove email from my phone, turn off all social media notifications, use the "Do Not Disturb" option, and turn off Facebook Messenger.

Once I made this decision and got used to it (it did take time), I felt liberated. I was no longer tied to my phone. I could focus and was more productive. My mindset improved. Everything was better.

WHAT HAPPENS WHEN YOU SEE A NOTIFICATION?

According to Dr. Sanam Hafeez, PsyD, a licensed psychologist and professor at Columbia University in New York City, "The alerts from phones or even the anticipation of them, shuts off the prefrontal cortex that regulates higher-level cognitive functions, and instead, forces the brain to send emergency signals to the body."[24]

Yikes! No wonder we often feel stressed and distracted by our notifications. So why are we reluctant to turn them off? Because those notifications send dopamine to the "reward center" of our brains. "It's similar to feeling gratified, such as feeling a rush of winning at a slot machine, or eating a chocolate cake," says Dr. Hafeez.

So, notifications do two things to our brain: send emergency signals and falsely amp up our dopamine. Good times!

I know I felt this way when a notification came through on my phone. It was a jolt coursing through my body, and when the notification was for something I was anticipating, I felt exhilarated.

Think about what happens when you see a notification on your phone. Do you feel a sense of urgency? Or being rewarded? Maybe both?

Do you see how this can be controlling? I'm not suggesting you turn off text messages from your significant other, but how many notifications do you really need? Are these notifications worth altering your brain?

These are all personal decisions, of course. Hopefully, with this information in your back pocket, you will evaluate your need for notifications and think of how you can loosen your dependence on them.

SOCIAL MEDIA

Y ou absolutely, without doubt, need to create boundaries around your social media use. Here's what those boundaries should consider:

- What you want to see in your newsfeed
- How much time you want to spend on social media
- What you post on social media
- Who you want to interact with on social media

Let's break down each of these boundaries some more.

BOUNDARIES AROUND YOUR NEWSFEED

Facebook, Instagram, Twitter, even Pinterest have "feeds"—a river of information curated for you by the social media platform. Each platform has an algorithm, based on your interactions, engagement, and who you like and follow. It may feel like the social media sites have exclusive control over what appears in your feed (because the formula behind the algorithms is unknown, so we are guessing how they work). Here's the thing: *You do have control over your newsfeeds.* How? By creating boundaries so your newsfeed shows you *exactly* what you want to see.

The best way to see your desired newsfeed is to interact with people and companies whose content you want to consume. Leave comments, make a reaction, and share. These actions tell the social media platform that you like this content, and the platform will put more of this stuff in your feed.

Especially on Facebook, you can stop individual ads from showing in your newsfeed (I do this all the time because I often see the same ads repeatedly). You can unfollow people and pages whose content you don't want to see. Also, you can search the Internet without logging into Google to protect your privacy, so you do not see ads from the store whose website you just visited.

Also for Facebook, you can download Chrome extensions to help you filter out content based on keywords you set. So, if you don't want to see any posts about Christmas, you add "Christmas" as a keyword in the filter, and voilá! No more Christmas!

The key here is to learn more about the social media platform, its privacy settings and tools, and how you can manage your newsfeed better. You are in charge!

BOUNDARIES AROUND TIME SPENT

I'll be the first to admit that I can go down a Social Media Rabbit Hole. I have caught myself mindlessly scrolling through Instagram, Facebook, and Twitter on more than one occasion. Don't even get me started on Pinterest and YouTube!

Mindless scrolling is a time waster and a signal that I am procrastinating on something. It's not the best use of my time.

I will not tell you how much time to spend on social media. If you are an entrepreneur like me, you spend time on social media to market your business, run Facebook groups, host Instagram Lives, and upload vlogs to YouTube. These activities take time!

Plus, it's wonderful to see a picture of your college roommate's daughter in her Halloween costume or to reconnect with a long-lost cousin. For sure, social media has a silver lining.

However, social media can be unhealthy. It can raise your blood pressure. It can make you hate your friends and relatives for posting stupid shit. This is why you need a time boundary. How you set that is up to you—just give yourself permission to do so. Your mindset will improve, you will like people more, and you can finally finish reading that book on your nightstand.

BOUNDARIES AROUND WHAT YOU POST

What topics will you not post about on social media? If you haven't thought about this, I encourage you to make a list of off-limit topics. Go deeper than "no politics or religion." What about politics won't you post about and why? What about religion won't you post about and why?

These are personal decisions. There is no right and wrong. When you have thought about off-limit topics, you will have the courage to say to yourself, or to someone else, "I don't talk about this on social media."

Beyond politics and religion, other off-limits topics might include showing where your kids go to school, telling people where you go to church, talking about work, and sharing other people's health updates.

You are in charge of what you post. Don't be influenced by what others are doing. If they want to show the world everything, that's their choice. It doesn't have to be yours.

BOUNDARIES AROUND WHO TO INTERACT WITH

Who do you want to interact with on social media *by platform*? For example, on LinkedIn, do you want to interact with people from every place you worked? On Facebook, do you want to friend people you met once at a conference?

This boundary can be the hardest for women because we are innate people pleasers. However, your Inner People Pleaser is not in charge of your social media.

Here's the mindset shift you need to embrace: *A social media friend is not the same as an off-social media friend.*

Let me explain: As an entrepreneur, I get Facebook friend requests from people who do not know me. They may know some of my friends, which often inspires them to request to be my Facebook friend. I never accept it. They are not my friend. Maybe we will be in the future, but today, they are not my friend, and I have a strict boundary that my personal Facebook profile is filled with friends.

It's important to wrap your head around the term "friends" as it relates to social media. A social media friend is just a marketing term created by Facebook. It is not an actual definition of a friend. Sure, there are some wonderful people on Facebook who could become your friends, but I doubt they will be the ones who rescue you if your car breaks down, or who won't judge you if your kid gets in trouble at school.

Fans, followers, and friends are monikers to represent people you can interact with on social media. That's it.

Now, let's talk about "unfriending" and "unfollowing" because these are two important boundary-making activities on social media.

You have permission to unfriend. You have permission to unfollow. All these actions mean is that you don't want to see this person's content in your newsfeed. That is all. It does not mean that you are a terrible person, or that you hate the other person, or you will now spend your afterlife in Hell because you unfriended someone.

It just means you don't want to see their stuff.

You don't have to explain why and you don't have to apologize. You are setting a boundary and controlling the content in your newsfeed. That is all.

I do this all the time. Here are some reasons why:

- I disagree with their political ideology, and they *only* post stuff about their political ideology.
- I don't want to see their business stuff on their personal

Facebook profile (this is against Facebook's Terms of Use, by the way).

- I am sick and tired of seeing their baby. I know! This is horrible! But if you post 35 pictures of your baby every day, in separate posts, then I will unfollow or unfriend you. I don't care how cute your baby is. The repetition feels like water torture. Side note: This is why my dog has her own Instagram account. Otherwise, I would be the one posting 35 pictures a day of my basset hound.

None of this means I hate the person, or don't support her business, or don't think her baby is cute. It just means I don't want to see it in my newsfeed.

Loud Woman, you have permission to create these boundaries for your social media use. Your sanity and mindset rely on you doing so. Don't be a pawn to social media and the companies who run them. You are Louder than that!

25

TIM AND DENISE

I wanted to contact Tim Ferriss (author or *The 4-Hour Work Week*) to ask that he join my book club discussion. I went to his website and found his "Contact" page,[25] and what I discovered was pure Boundary Genius.

His contact page had the following sections:

- *Media and podcast sponsorships:* He pointed to a webpage with his approved images and shared a form for podcast sponsorships. He also said "I am not giving out media interviews at this time." Done. Period.
- *What else he's not doing right now:* Here, the boundaries were super clear as Tim listed out what he was not doing at that moment, including product testing, speaking engagements, and book blurbs.
- *Book-related questions:* He referred to his blog and its search bar, and encouraged his readers to look through his vast article library.
- *How to ask him a question:* He said to send him a tweet or comment on his blog with a promise to respond. Tim also

linked to a couple Facebook groups where you could post your question for his community to answer.

Did I think Tim was an asshole for having such clear-cut boundaries? No. I appreciated his instruction. I got the answer to my question and proceeded to send him a tweet. Done and done.

Now, you may be thinking, "But Tim is a guy and can get away with this!" We know that people respect a man's boundaries. So, can a woman do this? *Absolutely.*

Meet Denise Duffield-Thomas, a money mindset mentor for women. Her Contact page is also pure Boundary Genius. [26]

The first line on her Contact Page says this, "Omg, can I tell you how much I hate email?" Then, she had a short FAQ section with gems such as how to get Denise on your podcast, how to hire Denise for a speaking gig, and how to troubleshoot the log-in for her courses. In addition, her FAQ set up firm boundaries about contacting her to say hi (do it on Instagram), sending her your book (send it to someone else), and how to mail her a gift (please do not).

Her Contact Page is honest and clear, and that's what boundaries are all about.

26

UNBENDABLE

W hen I first started working full-time in my business, I was excited to be working from home (a dream of mine for years). I was tired of commuting. I was tired of following someone else's schedule. And working from home felt like a great way to manage personal time commitments. I could not find an employer to allow me to work from home, so I started a business where I could.

I do not know what it is about working from home, but some people think you have all the time in the world. Like you're eating bonbons and watching *The View* every day.

When I first started working from home, I did not think twice about talking to my mom in the middle of the day, or helping my parents get to the doctor at a moment's notice, or driving my kids to and from school (even though the bus stop was at the corner).

It did not take me long, though, to realize that I cannot work in this boundary-less environment. I needed boundaries—both in space and time.

So, the kids started taking the bus (begrudgingly). I split medical appointment duties with my siblings.

And then I had to deal with my mom.

Mom did not like my boundaries. She called me during the day, sometimes multiple times, always leaving voice mails that I needed to call her back "right away." One time, when I was on a private coaching call, she came to my house and knocked on my front door. When I didn't answer, Mom walked to the back of my house and banged on the other door. I had to ignore her knocking, though it broke my heart to do so. It reminded me of when I would let my kids cry themselves to sleep. It hurt and it was uncomfortable, but it was necessary.

Mom refused to accept that even though I was home, I was working *and* unavailable. Just like when I worked at corporate, I could not have visitors drop by or take a lot of personal phone calls.

It took years, but Mom finally understood. She calls in the evening now, unless it's an emergency.

Let me repeat: I took *years* of me not bending my boundaries for Mom to finally respect them. I was not asking for a lot—the same respect she paid me when I worked in corporate, and the same respect she extended to my siblings when they worked in their offices. She felt entitled as my parent, though, to unlimited access to me, and it is hard to undo that entitlement once someone feels it. The only thing you can do is to stick to your boundaries, even if it upsets someone you love.

There's an Internet meme that reads: *The only people who get upset about you setting boundaries are the ones who were benefiting from you having none.*

Now that's a truth bomb.

Before you set boundaries, you have probably allowed someone to take from you endlessly. Whether it's a loved one, friend, client, colleague, or boss, this person is a taker. Takers love to take and feel entitled to take from you.

Imagine a store existed where you could go any time of the day, grab what you need, and not pay for it. Pretty cool, right? Now imagine what would happen if this store established store hours and added prices to items. For a taker, this would annoy the hell out of her. She's thinking: *What the heck? I've been able to shop here any time, day or night, and get my stuff for free. How dare you change your policies?*

Well, that's how a taker feels about you. You are open 24/7 with free stuff. Now that you have boundaries, the taker is pissed because she doesn't have unlimited access to you (something she feels entitled to).

Remember, you are not a 24/7, free-for-all store. You are a human who is worthy of boundaries. It's hard (I know!), but your mindset depends on it.

Sometimes your Loudness will upset others. Your job is to stick to what's important (and yes, boundaries are important) and do so unapologetically. They will be okay, I promise.

27

HOLD 'EM

S o, you've set your boundaries: now what?

Here comes the hard part: Holding your boundaries. As we just talked about, others may hate your boundaries, and they may tell you they hate it, or just try to break them. It's your job to be Loud and protect the boundaries you created.

To hold your boundaries, you must communicate your boundaries. Take a look at these examples:

- If you're an entrepreneur, explain how people can contact you on your "Contact Us" page on your website. Just like Tim and Denise did. Both entrepreneurs are clear with their boundaries, and you can be too.
- Think about how you want people to contact you. Is it okay if they call you out of the blue? Is it okay if they send you a text message or Facebook message? How quickly will you respond to them? Once you've made these decisions, tell people so they can start getting used to your boundaries.
- If you're a parent, what boundaries do you need to set with your kids? For example, if your bedroom door is closed, can they walk in without knocking? How about texting you

during the work day? Again, once you decide, communicate with them. This is especially important if you work from home. Even a simple sign on your office door is helpful.

What happens if someone tries to violate your boundaries? You need to remind them about your boundary. You may feel uncomfortable doing this because you may upset the person. Remember, your boundaries exist to protect you and your happiness. The other person will get used to it *and be okay.*

I have a boundary with my students about contacting me through direct message, text message, or phone calls. The boundary is "only email me." I am blessed to have many students in Celestial University, and if they reach out to me in various ways, I lose track of their messages and risk not getting back to them. So, I request they email me so I can have their communications in one spot.

Sometimes, a student will forget and send me a direct message, and when she does, I don't answer her question. Instead, I ask her to email me. Here's how this conversation usually goes:

Student: Hey Jill, what do you think of adding an extra hour to Study Hall?

Me: Hey! It's great to hear from you! I would love learn more about your idea. Can you please email me at jill@celestialuniversity.com and share your thoughts? Also, just a reminder for the future, please email me with your questions or concerns. I don't want to miss your message!
Thank you!

Student: Okay, will do!

What if it's a "high-stakes" person, such as your boss or client, who keeps violating your boundaries? Always remember: *You are worthy of your boundaries.* Maybe set up a "three strikes and you're out" policy—whatever works for you.

Just know that when you respond, you are perpetuating the violation of your boundary. You are telling this person, "I know I have a boundary that I've communicated to you multiple times, but, because I'm responding again, I am telling you it's okay to violate my boundary."

Read that last sentence again. I know it may sting, but that's what is happening. At some point, you have to decide: *What is more important: My boundary (sanity), or being nice to this person?* I hope you'll choose the former. You can't pour from an empty cup, and when you allow people to violate your boundary, it's like you drilled a hole at the bottom of your cup.

Holding your boundaries is a crucial milestone on your Loud Woman journey. It's saying to yourself and the world that your happiness is important, and that you deserve the sacred parameters you have put around your life, energy, time, and money. What a beautiful way to express your Loudness!

28

ADJUSTMENT

Sometimes, though, you may need to adjust your boundaries.
I know, I know: I just wrote you must uphold your boundaries, especially as people push against them.

I promise I am not changing my tune, but sometimes, you cannot anticipate the result of your boundaries. So, you have to adjust them.

I once created a boundary around my work calendar where for two weeks out of the month, I would not take client calls or teach classes. These two weeks "off" would give me time to write content and work on my marketing plan. As I blocked off my two weeks, I shuffled my calendar around to squeeze in all my commitments during my two client-facing weeks.

This meant calls filled those "on" days. I worked my ass off for two weeks, coaching and teaching, and depleted my energy. Guess what? By the time my "off" weeks started, I could not do anything.

Seeing how this boundary was counterproductive, I tried something else. I adjusted my boundary to where I was not on the phone on Mondays and during the last week of the month. I could almost hear my calendar heave a sigh of relief. It was no longer buckling under all those appointments squeezed into every time slot.

Now, phone calls and classes do not fill my days. Seeing each day with just one commitment felt like a pile of bricks lifted off my shoulders. And because I managed my time this way, I had the energy to keep working on my off-the-phone days. I was more productive and energetic.

Is it possible you have to adjust your boundary because it's too strict? Of course. I caution you, though, to consider the consequences first. You established that boundary for a reason. We are all human, so you may have created a boundary out of anger or spite (both good reasons to reconsider your boundary). We also make mistakes, and as we try to enforce the boundary, it creates an unintended consequence that causes more harm than good.

You don't want to boundary yourself into a corner, plus we are discovering more about what makes us happy every day, which means our boundaries will need adjustment from time to time. Just make sure you adjust boundaries for *your* happiness, not someone else's.

MANNERS

If the foundations of good manners are caring for others' comfort, listening more than you speak, and glossing over the poor manners of others, having "good manners" actually grossly disadvantages women.

— ALICE WILLIAMS

29

DOG PARK

F ifteen basset hounds surrounded me that warm June morning. I was in my happy place at a Tampa Bay Basset Hounds meet-up. On this particular Saturday, we gathered at a dog park in Spring Hill, Florida—a beautiful dog park canopied by oak trees and dotted with dog agility equipment.

My friend Shawna and I co-founded Tampa Bay Basset Hounds, and every month, we travel to an area dog park and gather the bassets. If you have never seen twenty basset hounds playing together, imagine twenty long noses, forty long ears, and eighty short legs all running, chasing, and barking at each other. There's a lot of sniffing, as well as wrestling, slobber, and dog poop. I promise: It's a sight to behold!

My basset hound, Trixie, is super active, especially for her breed. She loves to play with her basset friends, especially her half-brother, Warren.

Warren and Trixie have a special, close bond, and if there ever was a WWE for dogs, they would be the stars. Their antics include hurdling over each other, taking the other one down, fake bites, and the weirdest noises ever emitted from domesticated animals. When people unfamiliar with Trixie and Warren watch them play, you can see the *wonder* in their faces. Not wonder, as in "this the most amazing thing," but rather, "I wonder if they should be separated."

I will admit it: Trixie is a bit crazy. While Warren enjoys a wrestling match, not all dogs do, and Trixie has learned to read the signals given by her basset friends. A dog will let another dog know when he's not interested, and the other dog gets it. With that said, most dogs who go to the dog park are ready to rumble, and if spats arise, they're usually caused by a human, which leads me to my story.

During this meet-up, a man entered the dog park, coaxing in his dog, who had her tail between her legs, and wore a submissive look on her face. As they entered, the bassets waddled over to say hi, and this poor dog was terrified. We quickly pulled the dogs away so she and her human could safely get inside the park.

A few minutes later, I heard the man hollering, and his voice was filled with anger. "No biting!" he said. Trixie was in the pack near his dog, so Shawna and I high tailed it over there to grab our basset hounds.

"Whoever's dog this is," the man shouted as we approached, "I'm going to kick it in its mother-fucking head!"

This man of at least 200 pounds was pointing at Trixie, my thirty-five-pound basset hound puppy.

The rage emanated from his like heat off concrete on a blistering summer's day. I thought for sure lightning bolts would shoot from his eyes, aimed directly at Trixie.

Stunned, I went into "fight or flight" mode and snatched up Trixie. I didn't say a word; I just escorted my puppy to the front of the dog park, away from this man and his seething rage. My friend, Shelley, collected Trixie in her arms, as I processed what just happened. *Did a man just threaten to kick my dog in the head? What type of person does that?*

Now, if I was fully within my Loud Woman Wits, I would have turned around and stood up for myself—and for Trixie. Frankly, if you threaten to hurt a dog, you are pond scum to me, and this guy deserved a good talking to.

Instead, though, my Polite Wits were in full effect. You know when you become polite and submissive to a man to diffuse a situation? It's my go-to tool, learned from a previous abusive relationship.

I walked over to this man and smiled. I asked for his dog's name, and I shared that my dog, Trixie, was the one who had upset him. I then apologized—even though I had done nothing wrong. I just wanted him to stop being angry.

It worked, I guess, because his anger subsided. He then launched into a full-blown explanation of why he was angry, saying he was over-protective of his dog because she had been bitten at this same dog park. I continue to concede, agreeing that it was good to be vigilant. And then I explained at great length how Trixie would never hurt his dog.

As I tell you this story, I am now flooded with regret. This is not how a Loud Woman should react. This is how a woman who has been silenced reacts. This jerk just threatened to kick my sweet dog in the head, and I'm talking to him like *I* did something wrong—all in an attempt to calm him down and diffuse the situation.

My smile and soothing voice are quick-deployed tools that I call on when I am scared. And in previous situations when I was scared by a man, this is how I escaped unscathed.

If I could redo this situation, I would have told this guy it was unacceptable to yell at my dog and threaten to hurt her. Period.

Thankfully, one of us had her Loud Woman Wits about her, and that was my friend, Shelley.

As this man and I returned to the front of the park, Shelley and Shawna were waiting. This guy, once again, explained how his dog was bitten at this same dog park before.

He no sooner put the period on the end of his sentence, when Shelley looked him, dead in the eye, and said:

"That's no reason to be hostile." No quiver in her voice, no hesitation, no apology.

He paused for a moment. I thought he would apologize. Instead, he announced his departure, taking his still-anxious dog with him.

I am grateful for Shelley's unapologetic, bad-ass-woman response to his story. That's how a Loud Woman does it. She ensured this guy didn't leave the dog park thinking his behavior was acceptable.

But here's something else Shelley did: She stepped into the gap left by a woman who couldn't muster her Loud Woman Wits at that moment. Shelley spoke up when I could not. And she did so without explanation or apology, and did not worry what this guy thought. Shelley took up the space she needed to let this guy know he was a jerk. That's how you do it as a Loud Woman.

GOOD GIRL

Good girl!" How many times have you been complimented this way?

What are seemingly nice words are loaded with patriarchal expectations about how we are supposed to behave: be polite, follow direction, be quiet, sit still, and do not disagree.

Let's face it: What constitutes "good manners" for girls and women are outdated, especially if you compare them to the expectations for boys and men.

Loud Women recognize this and know it's time to create our own rules about how we should "behave."

Make no mistake: Creating new rules about "manners" for women will not be popular. You may resist, too. *What's wrong with having manners? What's wrong with following direction?*

On a surface level, nothing. But when you crawl through the weeds of what constitutes a "good girl," you will see these good girl manners for what they are: *ways to oppress us.* In other words, good girl manners stop us from living life to the fullest.

In this section, we will tackle topics such as apologizing, being polite, taking up more space, interruptions, and showing emotion.

As you read, you may feel uncomfortable—even defensive. This is normal. I encourage you to keep reading. As the discomfort rises, journal about your feelings. Give yourself permission to explore this topic, turning over all stones, and see where you end up. I think you will realize you have been bound by societal expectations that do not serve you.

YOU SHOULDN'T HAVE SMILED
AT HIM

When I was a college freshman, I volunteered to teach adults how to read. Once a week, some classmates and I would go to an adult education center to work with their students.

When we arrived, we signed in on a clipboard, printing our names and phone numbers, so the center could track our hours for our college. Then, we would work two hours with the adults in the learning lab, celebrating their victories and learning about their lives.

One day, I sat at the bottom of a small stairwell, waiting for my fellow volunteers so we could head back to campus. A guy about my age sauntered down the hall, approaching me, and I thought he may need to get by. I jumped up and said, "Oh sorry, I'll move," with a smile.

The young man stopped in his tracks and whistled—like a cat call from a construction site. Immediately, discomfort engulfed me. I scrambled through the nearest door, and he followed me in. He stared at me, as if he was disrobing me with his eyes.

Did I stop his behavior? No, I just wanted to diffuse the situation. So, instead of sticking up for myself, I used polite manners as my defense mechanism: "Have a good day!" I said with a small smile.

The next week, when we came back to the learning lab, this guy was waiting for me. He watched as we signed ourselves in. He asked for my name, and I quickly said, again with a nice smile, "Sorry, I don't have time to chat. I have to start volunteering now."

I hoped he would get the hint and go away. I spent the next two hours looking over my shoulder. I put my friends on high alert too. They giggled and advised, "You shouldn't have smiled at him!" Thankfully, the morning was uneventful, and I remember sitting in my friend's car, feeling relieved, as she drove us back to college.

Later that day, the volunteer coordinator called me, asking me if I have been talking to a young man at the adult education center. I told her the whole story of how I should not have smiled.

She then told me this young man called another volunteer from my college. He had looked at our sign-in sheet and guessed which of the volunteer's names was mine. He took down an incorrect name and phone number, and called, reaching one of my classmates instead. My classmate thought something was off, so she called the volunteer coordinator to let her know.

The volunteer coordinator assured me I was safe and that the adult education center would deal with the guy. The whole time she was speaking, my friends' advice kept chanting in my head: *You shouldn't have smiled at him.*

As women, we should never fear our smiles. Really the advice should be to men: *Women's smiles are not permission slips.*

My smile was a defense mechanism. I knew something was off with this guy as soon as I locked eyes on him. Instead of appearing rude by telling him to knock it off, I smiled to diffuse whatever bomb was ticking. I smiled because I felt endangered.

Women have been taught that polite manners are a great way to avoid conflict. Being polite is a defense mechanism. We use our polite ways to diffuse tempers, especially when we feel threatened.

Here's the thing: Avoiding conflict may be easier, but it is not always the right thing to do. For example, when a woman is sexually harassed at work, she may politely ignore those initial advances, hoping her harasser will get the hint and move on. These polite manners, though, can embolden her harasser. He may continue to harass the woman because she chose to be polite instead of telling the guy to knock it off.

Being polite has its place, for sure, in our society. We should say please, thank you, you're welcome, and I'm sorry when the situation calls for it. How can you tell when manners are the right response? By the way you feel in the situation. If you feel uncomfortable in any way, it is a signal you are being threatened, harassed, or disrespected. Instead of falling back on polite manners, what would happen if you firmly told someone to stop? Or leave the situation without explanation?

To this day, I rely on using polite manners as a way to stay safe. It is a terrible way to live, truth be told, because you are not being yourself, you are not honoring your boundaries, and you are saying: *I am not worthy of sticking up for myself.* You are accepting that you are not worthy of feeling comfortable, which is *not* what a Loud Woman does.

Loud Woman, I challenge you and me to stay in our power, by permitting us to not be polite in every situation. You do not need to be polite when someone is making you uncomfortable. If you are like me and stay in the polite lane to influence what others think about you, abandon this thought. If you are being polite to calm someone else down, knock it off. Your discomfort is as important as the other person's feelings. You deserve to be comfortable. When someone else is making you uncomfortable, you have permission to abandon those polite manners and stick up for yourself.

Being polite is a choice. It is not compulsory in every situation, no matter what society thinks. Will this be hard to abandon? Absolutely; I am living proof. But if we can acknowledge the first step — accepting that being polite all the time is not okay — we will be on our way.

Do not be polite to avoid conflict. Do not be polite when you are uncomfortable. You deserve to be treated with respect in every situation.

32

BANANAS

I am an efficient grocery shopper. I make a list in order of the store aisles and order my deli items in advance. I go first thing on Sunday mornings to avoid crowds. This sometimes means I have to bag my own groceries, and that's okay with me. It's worth it to get in and out of the grocery store as quickly as possible.

Despite my efficiency though, sometimes I have to make an extra trip to the grocery store. Usually it's because I need more bananas.

These banana runs always occur in the afternoon, which means the grocery store has more shoppers. One day, as I beelined to the bananas, I spied a woman and her grocery cart in front of the banana display. I stood along the side of the banana display and reached over to grab a bunch. When she saw my hand, she immediately called out, "Oh, I am so sorry!"

I jolted in surprise. I almost wanted to look around to ensure she was speaking to me.

I smiled at her and said, "What happened?"

"Don't mind me. Just daydreaming and blocking the bananas!" she giggled.

I got it. She had the audacity to shop for bananas at the same time as me, and she was sorry for being in my way. This is a regular occurrence at the grocery store.

"No need to apologize!" I assured her.

She smiled again and pushed her cart away.

My fellow banana shopper made me sad, though. Why should she apologize for shopping for bananas? She was there first, and she was not in my way.

If I ever see her again, I hope she will stand in her power and grab bananas unapologetically. She does not need to cower, or giggle, or think she's less than in any way. Equally important, she does not need to apologize for shopping, or standing, or pushing a grocery cart.

So many times, women say "I'm sorry" in situations that do not require an actual apology, like these:

- You are a few minutes late to a meeting, and you say, "Sorry I'm late!" to your colleagues.
- Someone says something rude to you, and you reply, "I'm sorry; what did you say?"
- Someone bumps into you and you say, "Oh sorry! Didn't see you there!"

In these situations, you are apologizing for things that do not warrant an apology. It's how we are taught, as women, to navigate situations where we may have made someone unhappy. "I'm sorry" is said to diffuse a situation where you feel like you displeased someone.

One time at the end of a discussion call, one of my Celestial University students shared a vulnerable update about her marriage. She was upset and needed consolation, and we were happy to give her the space to tell us what was happening.

As soon as she finished her story, my student said, "I am sorry for dropping this on you all."

My student did not need to apologize. She was taking up the space she needed, allowing us to help her. However, because my student felt like she burdened us in some way (which felt like she made us unhappy), she apologized. I bet the apology just sprang from her mouth without much thought. That's because apologizing, even during situations that do not warrant it, are part of our good girl conditioning.

When you say sorry needlessly, you give up your power. As Loud Women, we need to stay in our power.

Yes, apologize when you hurt someone physically or mentally, or when you made a true-blue mistake.

Take a moment today to think about the times when you apologized. Did these situations *truly* warrant an apology? When you become conscientious about when you're saying sorry, you will maintain your power and Loudness.

Stop apologizing, Loud Woman. It's a critical part of being Loud.

33

EXPLAINING

When Rush Limbaugh passed away, Florida governor Ron DeSantis ordered that flags be flown at half-mast across the state. Rage engulfed me as I read his proclamation. Why were we honoring a man who effectively divided our country with his offensive, defamatory language?

I rarely speak about politics on my personal Facebook profile—mostly because I don't want to get into political debates—but I made an exception for this topic. I wrote, "Leave it to my state to lower the flags at half-mast to honor the death of a racist, sexist homophobe."

I knew I might get some push back, so I made a rule: *I don't have to explain my reasoning or my language choices.* With this rule, I waited to see who agreed with my sentiment—and who did not.

Almost immediately, someone who I used to work with asked: *Had I ever listened to Rush's shows?* I answered *yes,* but I did not drill down further. She accepted my answer and moved on.

Then came the next comment. "No you haven't! You listen to the media tell you what to think. Can you give any examples of his racism? I doubt it." This was from a man who I had met years ago when our sons played football together.

I took a deep breath, remembering my rule. I had given myself a permission slip to not explain. However, he just called me a liar on my personal Facebook profile, and that was unacceptable. So, here's how I responded:

"Please do not come on to my Facebook page and accuse me of lying. Unacceptable.

"I studied Rush Limbaugh, which included listening to his show, during my graduate studies at the State University of West Georgia, where I received my M.A. in history. My professor, who I studied Rush's show with, was Dr. Mel Steely, who was best friends with Newt Gingrich and his biographer.

"Additionally, I most recently researched Rush (again) as well as listened to his show as research for my new book, *Loud Woman*, which will be released by Highlander Press later this year.

"I do not have to provide examples of racism to you. It wouldn't matter if I did because you will believe what you want to believe."

See what I did here? I proved him wrong, without meeting his demand to prove Rush Limbaugh's racism. I also told him it was unacceptable to accuse me of lying.

After reading my comment, this man accused me of using my page to promote a book and still demanded examples of Rush's racism. I ignored him at this point, never responding to him again nor providing the examples he felt entitled to. I didn't have to explain my viewpoint to him or anyone else.

Loud Women do not explain. Now, let me explain. (The irony, I know...)

Yes, there are times when we have to explain things, such as when we are training a new virtual assistant or raising your child. We explain so others can learn. This type of explaining is necessary.

However, there are times when women explain because they are concerned about upsetting someone. This type of explaining in unnecessary, and just like when you apologize needlessly, you are giving up your power when you explain needlessly, too.

Let me give you an example:

A friend calls and asks if you want to go out to dinner that night. You had already planned to stay in and watch Netflix, and you are not in the mood to go out.

So, you launch into a lengthy explanation of why you can't go out (rough week in the office, got your period, need to shave your legs, etc.). Seven sentences later, you finally utter, "No, I can't go, but *thank you* for inviting me!" in a guilt-filled tone.

Get comfortable with saying "yes" or "no." Get comfortable with five-word explanations like "I have other plans tonight." As long as you are at peace with your decision, that's enough.

Explaining taps into our Inner People Pleaser. We do not want to ruffle feathers, we do not want to hurt people's feelings, and we do not want anyone mad at us. Furthermore, we feel guilty. So, we explain. Sometimes we use lies and half-truths to soften the blow. This means we are concocting a story to cover our shame. Wouldn't it be simpler to just say yes or no, and then move on?

Explaining is expected from women. Think about how a guy turns down a dinner invite. "Thanks, man, but I'm gonna stay in tonight." Boom! Done! No explanations about a hard week at work or the need to groom — just a simple "no thanks," and he's on his way to the couch and Netflix.

Here's the thing: He probably will not get too much push back either. Why? People will not challenge a guy about his decision. He made it, he gave his answer, and it's accepted.

If a woman does this, she will get follow-up questions. *Why are you staying home? Are you okay? Shouldn't you leave the house?* No wonder we are offering up half-baked explanations; we know the questions are coming.

The only way to stop the follow-up questions is to stop explaining. Take a page from a guy's book and tell your decision without explanation. If you get follow-up questions, don't answer them. Eventually, you will train your family and friends to accept your decision without further drilling.

Loud Woman, this may not be easy. This will go against everything you have been taught as a woman. It will feel like "bad manners," and you will worry that you upset someone. However, to keep your power, to maintain your happiness, and to secure your boundaries, you must stop explaining.

34

PAYCHECK LICKER

A young man approached my teller window on a Thursday afternoon. He was with his co-workers, cashing their weekly paychecks, as they did every Thursday. Most of his co-workers were older, hard around the edges and reluctant to engage in small talk. They wanted their cash so they could get on with their lunch.

Not this guy. His Thursday bank visit gave him more than cash in his pocket, it gave him an opportunity to make me uncomfortable.

I swear this guy reveled in it. Every week, he tried something new. A hard stare. A lick of his lips. Exclaiming "Is it hot in here?" while fanning his paycheck. His co-workers laughed and egged him on.

I hated to work the Thursday lunch crowd because this guy always harassed me. Worse, I felt like I had to tolerate this guy's behavior. He was a customer, plus an employee of a large account holder. So, I kept my head down and counted out their cash.

Every Thursday, I prayed for two things: He would be quiet, and another teller would have to serve him. Half of my prayers came true. He was always obnoxious with his inappropriate looks and gestures, but he never ended up in front of me.

Until the day he did. When he realized I finally would be cashing his check, he began a little show in line, seeking high fives and slaps on the back from his co-workers. You would think he was in line for a lap dance.

As my customer vacated the teller window, this guy waltzed up like John Travolta sauntering down the street in *Saturday Night Fever*.

"Hello," I greeted him.

"Why hello to you," he purred, holding up his paycheck. He put the paycheck to his mouth and licked the top of it like he was moistening an envelope flap. Then, he held it out for me.

I sat in disbelief. *Did this guy just LICK his paycheck and hand it to me?*

I half expected someone to jump out and proclaim, "Smile! You're on Candid Camera!"

My Candid Camera expectation evaporated just as quickly as it had appeared, and I still had to deal with this wet paycheck. I wrangled with my choices.

Good Girl Jill: Grab his paycheck, cash it, and get him out of my window as quickly as possible. He scares me. What if I upset him and he reports me to my manager? Or worse, what if he follows me to my apartment and does God knows what to me?

Emerging Loud Woman Jill: I am tired of this guy's bullshit and his sense of entitlement. Not to mention, I don't want his saliva anywhere near my body.

These thoughts raced through my mind as I stared back at him. He grinned and tapped his check on the counter.

It was the tapping that took me over the edge.

"I am not touching that," I said.

"You have to," he replied. "It's your job to cash my check."

Fear swelled up in my chest. *This asshole was not worth my job*, I thought.

"I am not touching it. It has your spit on it, and I don't have to touch it. If you like, I can get my manager to talk to you."

He tapped his check again on the counter and cocked his head to the side. "Last chance," he warned, as the grin dissipated from his face.

"Have a good day," I responded, and for the first time ever, I flashed him a pretty smile.

His co-workers could see and hear what was going on, and they began to rib him as he left the bank.

My moment of bravery passed quickly, and now fear filled me again. *Why didn't I just cash this guy's check?* I humiliated this clown, and now he could be a loose cannon.

After the lunch crowd dwindled, I spoke to my manager, James. I figured if I confessed my sins, he would just write me up, and I would keep my job. I liked James. He was a nice guy with funny stories and a quick wit, who, despite being a retired Army Ranger, was approachable. I felt it was best to confess my "sins" and move past the incident.

I hadn't intended to tell James the whole story of how I had endured inappropriate looks, gestures, and words, but as I explained that day's events, everything tumbled out. As I finished my horror story, I looked at James and braced for the worst.

James' face filled with pity, and he said, "Jill, I am so sorry you have been put through this. I'm glad you didn't cash his check."

He asked for the guy's name, which I reluctantly told him, and James said I had nothing to worry about. He would take care of everything.

And James did. Every Thursday, these men came into our bank, quietly and politely, including the Paycheck Licker. In fact, that guy never even looked at me or said another word about me. He also never stepped foot in my teller window again.

If I had not stood up for myself, I would have continued to be harassed. Not only did I stand up to the Paycheck Licker, I stood up for myself by talking to my manager. I was terrified to do both, but I did it. I am so glad because the harassment stopped and nothing further happened.

I was lucky this was some insecure guy who wanted to put on a show at my expense; God knows we have seen more tragic endings when women stand up for themselves. What I can say, with certainty, is this: I am glad I had the self-respect to open my mouth and demand better treatment. I could not predict the ending, but I could predict what would have happened if I cashed that wet paycheck. The ramifications for not speaking up were far greater than defending myself.

Am I perfect at this? Not at all. The incident occurred in my early twenties, and I still wrestle with defending myself now, as evident from my dog park story. With each incident, though, I get stronger, and my commitment to stick up for myself gets stronger too.

It is amazing how many of us put up with crap because we do not want to be impolite, or because we fear what might happen if we stick up for ourselves. The stakes can be so high.

Here's the thing: The stakes are high because we have allowed them to be. When we do not stick up for ourselves, we are telling the world that we have such low self-worth that jobs, relationships, and people's perception of us are more important. We have accepted a world where it is okay for a woman to be fired for telling a customer to stop harassing her. We have accepted a world where we allow cat calls on the street. We have accepted a world where friends can cut us down and then come back around when they need something from us.

We can unravel this, Loud Woman. If we all begin to stick up for ourselves, we will create a shift. People around us will realize that our self-worth is high, that we no longer live by the outdated rules of good-girl behavior, and we demand better treatment. They will realize we will no longer stay quiet, and if a woman is too scared to speak, another Loud Woman will step in and advocate on her behalf.

As long as we tolerate this behavior, the Paycheck Lickers of the world will always test us. When we speak up, they will stop. Women will be less scared to stick up for themselves, and the Paycheck Lickers will fear what will happen *to them.*

Loud Woman, speak up. Know it is not bad manners to stick up for yourself. You are worthy of the best treatment, the kindest words, the most fulfilling of relationships. And you can get all of this when you no longer tolerate anything less.

35

MANSPREADER

W ikipedia defines manspreading as "the practice of some men sitting in public transport with legs wide apart, thereby covering more than one seat."[27]

Manspreading violates your personal space because a man's legs encroach on your seating area. You have to wonder what kind of entitlement a guy has to do such a thing. Metaphorically, manspreading is just a way for men to take up more space in the world.

I once dealt with a "manspreader" on a flight home from New York. A young man fell asleep in the middle seat, with his legs and feet wide apart, leaving me about half of my foot space. I am almost six-feet tall with size 10 feet. I felt like a pretzel, trying to twist my feet and legs into the space he left me.

It was too long of a flight to put up with this shit, so I elbowed him in the ribs. He jolted awake and quickly readjusted his legs. Then I dropped my tray table and plopped my laptop on it, reclaiming my space so he could not invade it again.

My husband once explained to me that manspreading is not an intentional grab for space. It's just a comfortable seating position that men do without thinking.

I have no doubt that most men are not trying to be jerks when they are manspreading. They are trying to be as comfortable as possible in a too-small travel space.

Here's the thing, though: A man's first thought isn't *I wonder if the person next to me will get mad if I spread my legs and take up some of her space.* They just do it.

Most women can't do this—or more accurately are afraid to, especially if that requires encroaching on a guy's space.

Again, society has taught women to be differential and polite in public spaces, so we would not dream of sticking a body part in someone else's space. Often, we do not even use the arm rests, keeping our arms close to our torso. Women work hard at maintaining a safe bubble within the confines of our defined space. To tiptoe an inch over is not in our purview.

Would a woman ask a man to return his feet and legs to his space? Probably not. You do not know what the guy's reaction will be.

Loud Women, it's time to take up more space in the world. If that means some passive-aggressive, tray-table-down action on an airplane, then so be it.

This also means we need to assert more space in business, politics, and home. Think about ways you have experienced manspreading—and not just on an airplane or subway. How about in your shared bed? Or around a conference room table?

It is wrong for guys to feel entitled to our space, even if they do not intend to be jerks. You are right to demand a correction and claim your space, too.

So, put your tray table down, ladies. You have space to occupy.

I'M SPEAKING

On Tuesday, July 28, 2020, United States Attorney General William Barr testified at a House Judiciary Committee hearing about the Department of Justice's response to Black Lives Matters protests. Representative Pramila Jayapal began her questioning, and after Mr. Barr attempted to interrupt her, Jayapal said, "Excuse me, Mr. Barr, this is my time, and I control it."

It was a declaration heard around the world as women remembered all the times men interrupted them.

Yes, Loud Women, it is our time, and we control it.

Whenever we are engaged in a discussion—whether it's a casual conversation around the dinner table or a more formal conversation in a conference room—women get interrupted. Sometimes other women interrupt us, but mostly, the interrupter is male.

It does not matter who is doing the interrupting; what matters is that you do not tolerate it.

You will be interrupted for many reasons, from someone being passionate about the topic, or just being thoughtless, or wanting to argue with what you are saying. While many interrupters are not malicious, some have an ulterior motive.

What do I mean?

The interruption is an attempt to silence you. You are being too Loud, too wrong, too right—*too something*. It is irrelevant that you were not done finishing your thought. The interrupter, in the simplest of terms, wants you to shut up.

Loud Women don't tolerate that bullshit.

How do you stop being interrupted? This is where the rub occurs because you have to abandon those "good girl" manners. We are conditioned to be polite and differential, and to interrupt someone who is interrupting you goes against our conditioning. It feels rude, even though the rude behavior started with the interrupter.

Push through your good girl manner conditioning, and speak up, probably loudly, just as Representative Jayapal did while questioning Mr. Barr.

I was not finished.

Do not interrupt me.

This is my time, and I control it.

As you stop the interrupter, do not apologize. State that you have been interrupted and continue making your point. Do not rush, either. Your opinion, reflections, thoughts, and questions all matter, and the interrupter can wait for a natural break in the conversation to make his point.

This takes practice, and you may find it to be more comfortable to practice with family and friends. My husband is an interrupter. He does not interrupt to be malicious (thankfully), and it's given me ample time to practice saying, "You're interrupting me!" (Which is always met with an apology and space to finish my thought.)

Because I have practice at home, I have an easier time standing up for myself in other situations. So, look at friendly places to begin this practice, perhaps even telling your friends and family that you are working on this skill.

And if you're an interrupter, work on it. I interrupt people, and I get so annoyed when I do. My interruptions stem from impatience. I try to finish people's sentences or am too eager to interject my thoughts. I am working on not being an interrupter, and when I do interrupt, I make sure to apologize.

We are all learning here.

EMOTIONAL

I was blessed to have many wonderful aunts in my life as a child. My Aunt Jean was no exception. I called her my "Fairy Godmother," because I knew if she could, she would make my every dream come true. Aunt Jean dyed her hair—often bright red—and teased my mom about being the "bigger sister." An hour with Aunt Jean was filled with laughter. The last time I saw her, she grinned from ear to ear and called me her beautiful niece. She always knew how to make me feel loved.

When she passed away in 2014, Aunt Jean hadn't made preplanned funeral arrangements. My mom wanted to have a service for her sister, and she asked me if I could help find a minister. At the time I worked for a large healthcare system and asked the chaplain if he would officiate. He agreed, and on the day of Aunt Jean's service, he gave a beautiful sermon.

I am not much of a crier, especially in public. Sure, I will get teary-eyed from time to time, but I usually don't sob openly.

At Aunt Jean's service, though, I could feel a sob crawling up my throat. I tried to suppress it, not wanting to cry in front of everyone, especially the chaplain, who was a work colleague.

I managed to keep it together through the service, and at the end, I approached the chaplain to thank him for his beautiful words. As I spoke to him, my aunt's best friend approached. She gave me a hug, and as she pulled back, she looked me in the eyes and said, "Your aunt was always so proud of you."

That was it. I lost it. I could not hold back the tears, the sobs, the snot, anymore. I stood there, bawling my eyes out, not caring who saw me or what they thought. The grief exploded from me like a volcano.

The chaplain and my aunt's friend stood with me as I sobbed, rubbing my back, neither saying a word. They bore witness to my grief and honored it.

What was beautiful about this moment was the permission to be my most vulnerable self. I allowed myself to cry in public about my aunt. I dashed away thoughts that it was not okay to show one's emotions. It felt good to cry—just like it felt good to laugh at the precious memories of my Aunt Jean.

As for the chaplain, he did not judge me for crying. He certainly didn't tell others about it at work. While I have no proof, I like to believe he applauded it. Who wouldn't want to surround himself with people who aren't afraid to show their humanity?

How many times have you heard that a woman cannot be in a leadership position because she is "too emotional?"

It's an age-old and sexist way to keep women in their "place" because emotions and leadership allegedly do not go together.

We know this is hogwash, but watch what happens when a woman runs for office. What did people say about Hillary Clinton when she ran for U.S. President? She was called mean, angry, and vengeful (among other things). Coincidentally, people called her opponent Donald Trump similar names, but somehow, those were compliments. See the double standard here?

As a result, women have suppressed their emotions. What a shame. Why not be our true selves? If something makes you sad, cry. If something brings you joy, laugh. In fact, we should encourage men to show their emotions instead hiding behind a no-feelings mask. (I am so glad, though, that many men have embraced their emotions!)

Emotions make us better leaders. Imagine if politicians, police officers, and other authority figures could express their emotions. What a better world this would be.

Now, let's talk about anger, because there is nothing more scandalous than an angry woman, right? How many times have you seen a media report or a social media post defiling a woman because she expressed anger? What's wrong with being angry?

In her book, *We Should All Be Feminists,* Chimamanda Ngozi Adichie recalls the opinion of an acquaintance who had read her article about being young and female in Lagos, Nigeria. This person claimed Adichie's article was angry, and she should not have made it so.

"I heard the caution in the acquaintance's tone, and I knew that the comment was as much about the article as it was about my character. Anger, the tone said, is particularly not good for a woman. If you are a woman, you are not supposed to express anger, because it is threatening."[28]

An angered woman is often perceived as a threatening one. How are we threatening? I think it comes down to the difference between how some boys and girls are raised. Boys are often encouraged to show their anger and might, while girls are not. When a girl is angry, it upsets the boys because they feel like their right to be angry is somehow revoked.

If you are reading this and thinking: *Bullshit! I can get angry!* Let's take a moment to see what happens when women show their anger.

Look at the 2017 Women's March: How many people made rude comments about the marchers? How many media outlets condemned their anger? How many politicians wrote off the march as just a bunch of angry women?

Fox News contributor Steve Moore, for example, objected to the messages on the marchers' signs, calling them "putrid and vulgar," and upset to see so many young girls with such signs. "Call me a sexist, but I hold women to higher standards of conduct than men."[29]

Well, Steve, you are a sexist. There's nothing wrong with women using foul language and expressing their anger, even on poster boards.

Or look at what President Donald Trump said about environmental activist Greta Thunberg when she won 2019's *Time Person of the Year*:

"Greta must work on her Anger Management problem, then go to a good old fashioned movie with a friend!"[30]

Greta is angry that the planet she lives on is wasting away, thanks to bad human decisions (made primarily by men, may I add). Why shouldn't she be angry?

Here's the thing: Anger creates results, especially at a policy and cultural level. Anger is a window into what needs to be fixed. There's nothing wrong with being angry. What's wrong is that we are uncomfortable when women are the angry ones.

Loud Woman, you can get angry. In fact, please do. While you're at it, please be happy when you feel happy, be sad when you feel sad, feel jealous when you feel jealous—and whatever other emotion you are feeling. Yes, you are a Loud Woman, and thanks to your emotions, you are a human being, too.

FEAR

Living with fear stops us from taking risks, and if you don't go out on the branch, you're never going to get the best fruit.

— SARAH PARISH

38

9/11

I was thirty-six weeks pregnant when the plane hit the first tower on September 11, 2001. I put my hand over my belly as I watched the World Trade Towers fall, the burning Pentagon, and the remains of the plane crash in that Pennsylvania field. I wondered: *How am I going to raise my children in this world?*

Days later, the stories about the victims poured in. With rapt attention, I listened as loved ones shared their final phone calls made from airplanes and desk phones. I learned about their ordinary lives. A mother who left a message on her family's answering machine, assuring them she was making her way out of the Tower, but never made it. The last known picture of firefighters, their last names stitched on their jackets, before they entered burning buildings—a testament to their bravery and duty. The flight attendant who took a shift for her colleague as a favor, not realizing she would be bound and gagged right after take-off. Their stories showed the depth of the tragedy, from people who thought that Tuesday would just be another day. My heart broke with each story.

Those stories amassed in my unconsciousness, and one night, months later, I had a vivid dream. I was in someone else's body on an airplane, realizing I was about to die. I am not sure how I knew about my impending death; perhaps I had learned about the other ill-fated flights and knew I was on one too. Dread filled every pocket of my soul. It felt like I was in a tunnel, with the faces of my fellow passengers spread along the periphery; some calm, others hysterical. I could hear reassuring words spoken to adults and children alike. Urgent, whispered prayers surrounded me.

I focused on the tray table in front of me and gripped my arm rests. I had so much life in front of me. I didn't even want to be on this airplane, yet here I was. And now I was going to die.

I then loosened my grip from the arm rest and reached out—maybe to the person next to me. I don't know because I felt an instant, intense heat, and then I woke up.

It's my belief that I experienced the final moments of a woman aboard one of those flights. I don't know who, but I will carry this person's experience, this vision, in my mind forever. I cannot describe the fear that ripped through me in that dream, leaving me breathless. My skin tingled, and my mind kept thinking how all of this was avoidable.

Several months later, I boarded an airplane to attend a work event in New York City, and months later, I took another flight to a family reunion. For these trips, I pushed that dream out of my mind with some success.

As the one-year anniversary of 9/11 approached, my mind amplified this dream. The emotions of the doomed passenger constricted my heart and would not let go. Thoughts of this passenger's powerlessness and regret plagued me. I imagined how easily she boarded the airplane that morning, trusting it would arrive safely at its destination. Instead, she was incinerated, becoming ashes that would never be reclaimed. I mourned for her.

What especially plagued me was her fear. Her fear enveloped me like a weighted blanket, and the more I thought about it, the heavier the blanket became—to the point where I could not kick it off.

I needed relief, and it came in the unhealthiest of ways: I vowed to never fly again. As soon as I decided this, the weighted blanket felt lighter.

For eleven years, I did not fly. I refused to go on business trips. I forced my family to drive to our vacation destinations. I thought people were crazy for getting on airplanes, which I then called "death tubes." I could not wrap my head around how they would voluntarily board an airplane that might crash.

In 2014, I signed up for an entrepreneur's business school based in Stamford, Connecticut. While most of the school work could be done at home, we had in-person meetings three times a year. For my first session, I asked my husband if we could drive to Connecticut. Bless his heart; he agreed. My family and our basset hound, Emma, climbed into our SUV and made the long trip from Florida.

While the trip was fun, it was more than 40 hours in the car. I knew I could not ask my family to do this again in four months. The time had come for me to face my fear of flying and get on a plane to Connecticut. I felt the panic attacks ready to spring forth, like a knight charging into battle. Even though the mere thought of flying made me nauseated, I decided it was time to do it anyway.

With four months to prepare, I began working on my mindset. I spoke to a therapist. I learned why people develop a fear of flying. I began to differentiate between possibility (yes, it's possible the plane could crash) and probability (it's not probable that it will). Most importantly, I visualized sitting on an airplane—*as me*, not as the person in my dreams. My visions showed an uneventful flight with a safe take-off and landing. I even visualized eating a bag of peanuts, how the salty flavor made me thirsty for the water in my small, airline-issued cup.

As the class date got closer, it came time to book my flight. I looked up flights into a small airport in Westchester, New York. As I surveyed my options, my chest felt like a stone was lodged in it. Fear overtook me, and I walked into my husband's office, and I said, "I can't do it." He looked up from his computer and smiled, "Yes, you can." With his assurance, I returned to my computer and made the reservations, telling myself that I did not have to board the plane—I could just buy the tickets. I stared at my name on that plane ticket, proud of myself for conquering this first step.

I continued my visualizations and studied how airport security worked. I spoke to others about their flight experiences. I told one of my classmates about my fear, and she promised to text me as I waited for my flight.

The day arrived, and my husband drove me to the airport, hanging out with me until it was time to go to the terminal. He bought me a gorgeous carry-on bag that I loved. We said good-bye, and I told myself (repeatedly) that I would see him again.

I breezed through airport security. Shoes off, body scanned, laptop restored—I arrived at the gate and sat down. I must have peed three times before boarding started. When my section was called to board, I rolled my cute carry-on bag down the ramp and stepped on to the airplane. I was greeted by the nicest flight attendant and resisted the urge to hug her.

Then I turned to my right and faced the long aisle of the plane. My heart pounded. It felt like the aisle was getting narrower, like that tunnel in my dream. I took a deep breath and headed to my seat, telling myself: *Your job right now is to find your seat, that's it.* And when I sank down into the seat, I almost cried. I made it. I got on an airplane and didn't pass out in the process.

I continued my deep breathing and prayed to Archangel Michael to protect the plane. I dutifully looked for the exits as the flight attendant's safety talk directed me to. Looking around, it seemed I was the only person glued to her instructions. The plane took off, and it didn't burst into flames. *Okay, maybe I can do this,* I thought.

The flight was uneventful, as most flights are. I even worked up the nerve to peek out the window as we circled the airport. I sent another prayer up for a safe landing, and low and behold, we landed without a hitch.

When I was a kid, passengers would clap when the plane landed. I guess this only happens now when the flight was eventful, because there was no applause when those wheels touched the runway. Trust me, though, there was a round of applause rippling through my body.

Here's the thing: I felt the most scared in the months, weeks, and days leading up to my flight. Sure, I panicked as I got on the plane, but once my butt was in a seat, I became grounded, singularly focused on getting through the flight. I remembered my visualizations—not those of the poor 09/11 passenger, but of *me*, flying to and from New York.

I may have been scared shitless, for sure, but I was also determined. I knew this was a watershed moment for me, and I was up for the task, in spite of the fear.

In class, I shared my story with others. One of my classmates declared, "Your business is about to take off—just like you on that airplane." I laughed but loved the truth of her statement.

When you get past the fear, you feel unstoppable. The bravery it takes to get you through that moment makes a deposit in your Courage Tank, fueling you for the next fear to conquer. I did the thing I was most scared of doing, proving that I could do anything. It's a feeling I will never forget.

39

EGO

F ear is part of life, and it's a signal you should pay attention to. Just like all feelings, fear is neither good nor bad. Fear comes in many stripes.

Fears, like when your survival instincts kick in when you hear an animal growl, are necessary to keep you safe and alive. This was helpful during the prehistoric times when leaving your family's cave could result in death.

Then we have the fears our Egos drop into our brains. Remember, your Ego wants you safe and secure. Thankfully, we can leave our homes without fear of a saber-tooth tiger attack, but our Egos have not caught up yet.

Think back to my 9/11 story. My Ego reverted to its prehistoric roots with my fear of flying. Getting on an airplane felt like Cavewoman Jill leaving her safe cave. Stepping on to that airplane felt like stepping into the woods where predators lurked. My Ego screamed, "Stay home! You're gonna die!" I had to recognize that my Ego, in an attempt to keep me safe, dispensed bad advice, and that it was irrational to fear dying in an airplane crash. Once I recognized my Ego's contribution to my fear, I had an easier time facing my fear of flying.

To untangle my Ego's response from Fear, I asked myself, "What is the likelihood that I will die in a plane crash? Is it probable or just possible?" Stopping to ask these questions grounded me to logic, which helped dispel the irrational fears bubbling inside of me.

As a Loud Woman, you will experience many different types of fears. The type of fear we'll address in this section are the ones produced by your Ego. The Ego-induced fears are meant to keep you small and safe —but that's not where a Loud Woman should be.

Before we talk about fear, I want to talk about your Ego for a moment. Your Ego has good intentions and is an extension of your True Self. In the past, I have dissed my Ego, even calling it Mr. Ego, often telling it to take a hike.

Truthfully, that's not the right approach. The Ego is not masculine or feminine. It should not take a hike because it's part of you and serves a valuable function.

Embrace your Ego. Show it some love and gratitude. It means well, for sure.

Then, make a choice: *Should I listen to my Ego right now, or should I thank it and press on?*

When it comes to Ego-induced fears, the answer most likely will be "press on." That is how you grow, get Louder, and live a more fulfilling life.

In this section, we will tackle different types of fears you may face as you get Louder, including a fear of success, fear of failure, and fear of criticism.

Don't try to avoid fear. That's impossible. Instead, let's learn how to recognize and honor your fear, and move in spite of it. This could mean you eliminate the fear all together. This also could mean you muster up enough courage to keep chipping away at your fear so it does not paralyze you.

However you approach it, you will feel better knowing how to tackle your fears on your Loud Woman Journey. Let's get to it.

FAILURE

T he first time I ever drove, I got in a car accident.

I was backing my sister's Sentra out of my driveway and did not realize I had to turn the steering wheel to avoid hitting Mom's truck. The result? I smashed my sister's Sentra into the truck's bumper. One minute of driving and I'd already had an accident.

I remember thinking, *how could you fuck this up, Jill?*

After the police officer left and the tow truck hauled my sister's car away, I ran to my bedroom and sobbed. I replayed the accident in my head, ruminating over every move I made and didn't make. I was a smart young woman—an honors student with a list of academic achievements—how could I get in a car accident on the first try?

If I could talk to my fifteen-year-old self, I would say, "Do not let this failure define you. You are meant to drive. Today, you learned a valuable lesson about driving. More importantly, you learned an important lesson about life. Just get back behind the wheel. You can do this."

I didn't bounce back from this failure too quickly. I resigned to the belief that driving wasn't meant for me. The crumpled hood of my sister's Sentra was all the proof I needed.

I spent the next four years bumming rides and avoiding the "you should learn to drive" conversation. I did not want to set myself up for failure again. Failing sucked. It hurt. It caused damage. I'd rather mooch rides than experience driving failure again.

And once I got my driver's license, I still told myself that I wasn't meant to drive. I avoided driving, especially driving other people around or going on busy highways. I sensed the next accident was just around the corner, waiting to pounce on me like a tiger hunting her prey. I figured the less I drove, the safer the whole world would be. I missed out on a lot because I wouldn't give myself permission to drive there.

Here's the thing: My first attempt at driving was an utter failure, but it wasn't the end of the world. Sure, it felt like it when the accident occurred, but if I had stopped for a moment and looked around, I would have seen that everything was okay. Instead of looking for proof of my inability to drive, I should have looked for proof that I could.

Thankfully, thirty-plus years later, I know this: Failure is okay. Failure brings lessons. Failure shows you how you can bounce back.

Many Loud Women are afraid to fail, but we have to try anyway, which can be hard in a world that demands perfection. It reminds me of that Internet meme about Ginger Rogers who did everything Fred Astaire did, but backwards and in heels.

Perfection is poured over us like our lives depend on it. We are expected to dance backwards and in heels—and feel grateful for being "allowed" on the dance floor. This stifling perception results in women not even trying, which may be the whole point.

First, let's move past our "failure is bad" mindset. Failure is not bad. Sure, it can feel like crap to fail, but it's never a bad thing. Why? Because of the lessons we learn from each failure.

Look back at the failures in your life. Did you learn something from each one? I bet you did. Those lessons shaped you into the woman you are today.

Here's a trick: Substitute the word failure for *lesson*; failing for *learning*. So, instead of saying, "I may fail at this," say, "I may learn from this." So much better, right? Words matter, and if "failure" globs up your brain, swap it out to *lesson* or *learning*.

With a newer mindset around failing, let's talk about why we fear failing.

Our society has long-engrained views on how women should look, talk, feel, stand, learn, parent, and love. Above all of these expectations is the big one: We are expected to be perfect. We must publicly look like we want all these plates spinning simultaneously—while donning a smile and pretty shoes.

Such high expectations! No wonder women are afraid of failure. The mountain we have to climb to success is so damn high. Men get to scale a hill; women get to scale Mount Everest. It's not fair.

Here's the thing: The only way our Mount Everest will change to a hill is if we bust through our fear of failure and do the things that frighten us anyway. Failure is not the end of the world. Let's embrace imperfection and stop avoiding failure.

As Maya Angelou said, "When you know better, you do better." Failing is part of the equation. We cannot grow without failure. Loud Women know this and move on.

41

THE TRAILER PARK

G randma, what happened to your hands?"
Grandma leaned over the sink, washing her bloody knuckles. As the reddish water circled down the drain, she chuckled, "Oh
honey, it's nothing. I had to clean the stove in the empty trailer, and I
skinned my knuckles on the side of the counter." She patted her hands
dry with a paper towel. Pink spots dotted the paper as she applied
pressure to her knuckles.

"I'm sorry you got hurt," I said, still concerned about the blood
oozing from her hand.

"It's what happens when you work hard," Grandma shrugged.

My grandparents owned a large trailer park in Holiday, Florida, and
I was the princess of the trailer park. I relished in riding my bike along
those gravel roads. Pebbles and shells flew from my tires as I raced
around, waving to my grandparents' tenants. For a five-year-old with a
bike and an active imagination, Anclote Acres was my playground.

While it may have been *my* playground, it was my grandparents'
livelihood. When they bought the land in the early 1960's, they spent
years clearing the land, building their home and outbuildings, and
placing trailers around the acreage. My grandparents did everything
from mowing the grass to pouring foundations, from looking for

tenants to cleaning up the trailers once the tenants left. They never hired anyone to help them; they did everything themselves.

If it wasn't bloody knuckles, it was the beads of sweat on Grandpa's forehead as he worked in the scorching Florida heat. If it wasn't the sweat, it was mediating quarrels between neighbors. If it wasn't the quarrels, it was the daily to-do list, which included chores on the weekend.

The trailer park brought great financial success to my grandparents, but they *toiled* to achieve it. It was hard, back-breaking work.

When I opened my business, I figured I had my grandparents' entrepreneurial blood coursing through my veins. About a year or two into my business, I realized something quite profound: *I had a significant fear of success.*

Specifically, my fears stemmed from my grandparents and how they ran their business.

My grandparents' entrepreneurial story fixed into my head as, "To be a success, you must work your fingers to the bone, and you will not have time for yourself."

To be sure, I want to be a success, but not to the detriment of my downtime or body.

I equated success to what my grandparents experienced—without considering that success could be different for me.

I began to visualize how my success *could* look, reminding myself that my grandparents' success story is not *my* success story.

I journaled about what my "perfect day" looked like as an entrepreneur. I visualized how I would serve my clients while enjoying time to exercise, play with my dog, write, nap, and read.

And when my Ego blasted the "if you succeed, your time will not be your own" song in my head, I responded, "Thank you, but that's not how it will be for me."

I then repeat my favorite affirmation ("It is safe for me grow"), and I continue to envision success on my terms.

Once I did this work, success started to come in the form of more clients, revenue streams, and creative ideas—without sacrificing my time, energy, or resources.

I think a fear of success plagues women more than we realize. Society has taught women to put our needs last, which could manifest into a fear of success. What if you have a successful career—will you still have time for your kids? What if you have a successful business—will you still have time to help your husband with his business? Will success make you less loving, generous, or charitable?

You can be a success and still be a wonderful parent, partner, friend, and neighbor. By allowing yourself the success you want, you're also allowing yourself to be a fuller version of yourself, which translates into a more fulfilled, happier mom, partner, friend, and neighbor.

It's okay to be afraid of succeeding (I think it's more normal than not). Acknowledging your fear is half the battle. Once you recognize it, bust through this fear and embrace your success.

42

ZITS

I t was the kind of day when you could see the heat radiate from the sidewalk. A well-dressed woman walked into the doctor's office where I worked, patting her forehead with a tissue. I smiled as she approached the window and noticed she represented a local home health care agency.

We made small talk as she passed over pens and Post-It notes. She complained about the heat, and laughed when I recommended that we play hooky and go to the beach instead.

When the laughter subsided, this woman leaned over the edge of the lobby window; her face straightened into one of great seriousness. I sensed she was about to tell me something profound—or even confide in me—so I leaned in to listen.

"You would be so beautiful if you didn't have acne. Have you tried Vitamin D?" she whispered.

My face, already red from dozens of pimples, deepened even more. "No, I haven't," I muttered.

She smiled at me, sympathy in her eyes. "Please look into it, okay?"

I pressed my lips together, forcing a smile, and nodded. She winked at me and took off, back into the heat.

I sat down in my chair, stunned. I was working alone in the doctor's office that day, which was a blessing because no one could see my embarrassment, followed by the tears of shame. Twenty-one-years-old, smart, skinny, beautiful smile, lovely hair—all the physical aspects of me that she could have complimented and she picks the one thing —THE ONE THING—that felt like a dagger lodged into my heart. My pimples, my acne, my zits. Whatever you want to call them, they have been my constant companion since puberty. Medicines, vitamins, sunburn—I had tried it all. My acne was persistent.

This woman's criticism of my acne, though disguised as "advice," was not just a comment about pimples on my skin. It was a commentary of how I was less than perfect. Indeed, it was a commentary about how I was *almost* perfect—so close, in fact—if I could only get rid of the zits on my face.

From that day forward, I worked even harder to eradicate my acne. I perfected how to cover up pimples with concealer and powder. I bought any and every product I could get my hands on. *I was so close to perfection, surely this product will make it so!*

For years, I stressed about my skin, spending a fortune on medications, procedures, and products, chasing the dream of perfect skin. Finally, in my late forties, I said fuck it. I would never have perfect skin. I stopped stressing about every little (or big) pimple. Sure, I still get zits, but I no longer allow my self-worth to be measured by how many blemishes I have (or don't have) on my face.

As you think about getting Louder, does a fear of criticism crop up? It is no wonder because many women dread being criticized for several reasons:

1. Women have an innate need to please everyone. Receiving criticism feels like we displeased someone, which feels uncomfortable.
2. Society values "good girls," the ones who do not cause trouble. If we receive criticism, we have rocked the boat.
3. We are burdened with perfection—looking, sounding, and dressing perfectly, especially in photos and videos. A

criticism about our appearance can be hard for us to move past.

You may never overcome your fear of criticism, but you can learn how to move past it. It's a huge mindset pivot because you must break years of societal conditioning. I do not want to discourage you, but it is important to know this unraveling may take time.

So, how do you move past it?

It comes down to this truth: *Someone's opinion of you is none of your business. Her criticism is a reflection of her, not you.*

When you receive criticism, I want you to remember the *mirror trick*. Imagine placing a mirror between you and your critic. Everything your critic says about you reflects back on her, *not you*.

One time, someone criticized me on social media because I turned down her application for my networking organization. She vented her frustration, accusing me of turning her away because of a scarcity mindset.

Now, I nearly internalized this criticism. I liked this person and felt like I let her down.

Instead, I visualized a mirror between us. The mirror reflected her feedback back on her, *not me*. When I did this mirror trick, it helped me process what she was saying. I found empathy for her. It also reinforced that I made the right decision about not approving her application.

In addition to the mirror trick, it's helpful to have healthy outlets for letting go of criticism. EFT (tapping), journaling, exercise, talking to a friend—these are all ways to let go of criticism and move on from it.

When you implement the mirror trick, coupled with healthy "let go" practices, you can move past your fear of criticism. You learn to shrug it off and move on. It takes practice and time, but if you shift your mindset on how you receive criticism, it will change everything in your life.

REJECTION

I didn't really want a new job, but I was tired of commuting. Sixty minutes each way took its toll on my car—and my soul.

I live in a suburb of Tampa, Florida, and most of the well-paying marketing jobs were not in my town, which meant I had to drive to the metropolitan area for work.

My kids were in elementary school by then, and I lost so much time in my car, mindlessly driving, when I could have been doing something with them—even if it was homework.

That's why I continued to receive job alert emails. What if something did open up in my small town? I wanted to be the first to know.

One morning, before beginning my commute, I checked my email and saw the daily digest of marketing jobs in the Tampa Bay area. I scanned the email, and much to my surprise, a local hospice listed a Director of Marketing position. What?!? Not only would this be a promotion from me, their main office was only twenty minutes from my house!

Impulsively, I emailed my team to let them know I was not feeling well and would not be coming into the office. Of course, I felt fine, but I wanted to submit my resume right away. I always tweaked the cover letter and resume for the job I was applying for, so I needed quiet time to write. Plus, if I got the job, who cared that I called in fake sick?

My cover letter and resume were masterpieces. I felt confident that the hospice would want to interview me. I submitted them and crossed my fingers. I needed this job; my sanity depended on it.

At the end of the work day, I received an email from the hospice's human resource department, asking for a phone interview. *Yes! I am on my way*, I thought.

I aced the phone interview, and the human resource manager set up an interview with the vice president. I scored a late afternoon interview for the following week, which gave me time to prepare my portfolio and my interview answers.

As I sat down in the vice president's office, I smiled with confidence, yet butterflies danced in my belly. *The stakes are high*, I thought. A local director of marketing job came along only once in a blue moon, and if I fucked it up, I wouldn't get another opportunity like this.

At the end of the interview, the vice president asked if I would agree to an interview with the hospice's CEO. I beamed and said yes.

I learned later that my interview wasn't solely with the CEO but would include a panel with other stakeholders, including physicians. While I was used to speaking to panels with my current job, I knew I could not falter even a little in the interview. They would sense it, and I would be out.

The receptionist escorted me to the conference room. Ten older men waited for me. I remember being shocked that not one woman, other than me, was present.

Truthfully, I don't think these men looked at my portfolio or resume until minutes before my interview. They didn't ask me questions about my current job or skills. They were more interested in learning about the growth strategy for the hospital I worked for. I did my best to answer their questions, but it was difficult to do so while shining a light on how I contributed.

As the interview progressed, I felt more and more crushed. I could not get ahead of the questions. I could see the job opportunity dissipating, right in front of me.

I emailed the vice president after my interview to thank him for his time. I carefully mentioned how I did not feel the questions focused on my abilities and contributions, and I told him I would be happy to speak to the group again if they had other questions. He wrote back (almost immediately) and said he would be in touch soon. I hung on to the glimmer of hope that he would say yes.

The vice president called several days later. He showered me with compliments, which perked up my hope. He then notified me that I did not get the job because they asked their previous director to return.

"Everyone thought you were a qualified candidate, but what we really wanted was for Jane to return. When they realized that, we decided to do what we could to bring her back on board," he said.

I was floored. I was expecting a "no thank you," but this rejection stung me in a way I did not expect. They took me through this entire process, just to reject me for their previous director (who resigned months before). Why didn't they do their best to keep her in the first place?

I had toiled to get that job. My resume, cover letter, and portfolio were the best I could deliver. I showcased my skills in the interviews only to lose the role the person who previously held the position. That hurt like a bitch.

Looking back, of course, I know it was a blessing to not get this job, but it didn't feel like it at the time. I felt stuck, sad, and dumb, repeating to myself: *I will never get a promotion. I will never stop commuting.*

I was so crushed by the rejection that I stopped receiving job alerts. If I couldn't get that job, I had decided I would never get one. I folded in defeat—just because of one rejection.

Thankfully, after several days, the sting subsided, but it took me years before I applied for another job. Imagine the possibilities I missed because I took that employer's rejection so seriously. I will never know, but I do know this: Rejection hurts, but it's not the end of the world. It's certainly not the reason to *not* do something.

What does rejection mean? In general, it's when someone is not interested in something you're offering, such as buying your business product or going on a date with you. When you are rejected, it feels very personal, as if the person is rejecting you (instead of rejecting what you're offering).

In her book *Playing Big*, Tara Mohr devotes a whole chapter to "Unhooking from Praise and Criticism." Why? Because women will not play a bigger game in their lives until they stop worrying what other people think about them.

In Tara's case, this obsession stopped her from writing for seven years. It was not until an inner voice told her to let go of what others thought. "You've got to give up on the 'love me, praise me' thing. You are going to have to do this in a different way than you've written in a very long time. You are going to have to write for you—for your joy, for your pleasure, for your self-expression, not for anyone else's approval."[31]

I am glad Tara listened to her voice because she's an amazing writer, and her book *Playing Big* continues to help me be a Loud Woman.

As a writer, I get where Tara is coming from, and this all stems from a fear of rejection. What if people reject what you write?

For three years, I wanted to write this book. And for three years, I let a fear of rejection stop me. Just like what Tara experienced, I didn't even want to start writing because I was afraid of what people would think. I was too concerned with praise and criticism, instead of writing for myself.

Luvvie Ajayi Jones made a similar statement in a Facebook Live she held to announce her second book. She encouraged all of us who wanted to write a book to write it for ourselves, and to let other people read it. That's the permission slip I needed.

Fear of rejection does not only affect writers, of course. How many times have women not asked for a pay raise, or applied to a certain college, or asked someone out for drinks after work? All the time. We are afraid of the "no" because we internalize it as "I am a failure." The "no" must mean I suck at my job, or I am stupid, or I am unattractive. We are stopping ourselves before we even start because we are afraid of what others may think.

Loud Woman, it's time to see your fear of rejection as what it is—a form of people pleasing, an extension of low self-worth, and a desire to stay safe and small. When you give into your fear of rejection, you are not reaching your potential. You are disregarding your intuitive nudges and settling for a life that is unfulfilling. It's time to stop it. Just as I wrote this book, you can do whatever you want to do, too.

The world will improve when you, as a Loud Woman, do things for yourself—for your pleasure, self-expression, or just because you want to. So, go do it. Sure, rejection may occur, but it's not the end of the world. It's just information. Do not let someone else's opinion stop you from being a Loud Woman.

44

DR. FORD

S he closed her eyes, raised her right hand, and promised to tell the truth.

Despite her vow, many already believed she was lying before she uttered one word of her testimony.

Why? Because Dr. Christine Blasey Ford had accused a man of attempted rape. And powerful people wanted this man to be a U.S. Supreme Court justice.

In a world where women are not believed, Dr. Ford became the bravest person I have ever seen. She testified despite the malicious comments being said about her, despite the death threats, despite having to relocate with her family.

She spoke because she wanted the American people to know what she knew—that Brett Kavanaugh was a sexual predator.

Dr. Ford kept the assault a secret for more than thirty years, telling only her husband and therapist. Only after Donald Trump nominated Kavanaugh for the Supreme Court did she reveal what Kavanaugh did to her; trying to keep it discreet at first, until it spiraled beyond her control.

Dr. Ford testified in front of Congress, recollecting painful memories of Kavanaugh's assault. Like many survivors, she did not remember every detail, such as the date or time of the assault, but she remembered his hand over her mouth and the fear that he would kill her.

She was so traumatized by her assault that when building her home, she insisted her bedroom have two exit doors in case she ever needed to escape from a bedroom again.

Dr. Ford and Judge Kavanaugh's testimonies are public record, so I will not rehash them here. Truthfully, it's still triggering to me, especially the rage expressed by Brett Kavanaugh. He felt so entitled to the Supreme Court appointment, like it was owed to him.

His spewing anger reminded me of so many men who could not, *would not*, let any woman get in the way of what he wanted. As I watched him berate Senator Amy Klobuchar, hot tears sprang to my eyes. I have been there, at the receiving end of gaslighting and verbal abuse. It fucking hurts, like a hot knife driven into your gut. Senator Klobuchar is tough, but you could see how taken aback she was by Kavanaugh's comments to her.

Yet, he still became a Supreme Court Justice, despite how his testimony showed he did not have the temperament for it.

And his confirmation shows what I know to be the truth: People believed Justice Kavanaugh over Dr. Ford, despite the evidence, testimony, and renouncements.

Just look at what people said about Dr. Ford. Accusations of her being a paid Democratic Party plant flooded social media. Others claimed she wanted to have sex with Kavanaugh, and he rejected her. My Facebook feed was filled with pure hatred for Dr. Ford, calling her a liar and a bitch. Some memes even suggested that men must be careful because any woman could accuse a man of rape and ruin his life. On and on the commentary went as if people were in that bedroom and watched what happened.

I could not even escape the vitriol at my local grocery store. While Congress deliberated the appointment, I overheard two male employees talk about Dr. Ford. One employee made it clear he didn't believe Dr. Ford because she did not report her crime thirty-five years before and "waited too long" to bring it up. The other employee agreed.

Which brings me to this conclusion: Many women will not get Louder because they fear people will not believe them.

You probably do not realize you even have this fear, but chances are you have been affected by a fear of people not believing you (or not believing *in* you). This "I don't believe you" fear can creep up in so many ways, such as:

- You want to pursue your true passion as a vocation
- You have a spiritual, telepathic, or intuitive gift
- You want to take on a new leadership role
- You want to write a book or speech about a trauma that occurred in your life

Sure, not being believed about sexual assault versus not being believed about your life's passion are opposite ends of the spectrum, but they are connected by this truth: *Society does not trust women.*

In the U.S., this is evidenced not only in sexual assault cases but in why the U.S. has not elected a woman president. It's also why we have a pro-life movement; many Americans do not trust women to make the best healthcare decisions for themselves and their unborn children.

The U.S. is not alone in this mistrust, which means women around the world are faced with the same predicament: *How do you get Louder when no one believes you?*

Here's what I want you to remember: The only person who has to believe you is *you.*

- If you believe you have a spiritual gift, you have a spiritual gift.
- If you believe you are ready to take on a leadership role, you are ready to take on a leadership role.
- If you believe you need to terminate your pregnancy, you terminate your pregnancy.

At the end of the day, you must be your best advisor. You must be the one who believes in yourself.

The fact that someone does not believe you is not your problem. Stay true to yourself and get Louder, and the naysayers will fall to the wayside (or you will get really good at ignoring them). Yes, people may not believe you, and that's okay. The only thing that matters is that you believe in yourself.

Remember Dr. Ford. She believed testifying about her attempted rape was the right thing to do. She did it despite the criticism she knew she would receive. That's how you do it, Loud Woman. That's how you do it.

45

IMPOSTER SYNDROME

L inda raised her hand during our Q&A call, and I could tell from the look on her face that she was feeling frustrated. An ADHD coach, she had enrolled in Celestial University because she wanted to attract more clients.

She asked, "Why would anyone hire me when they could hire someone younger or more qualified?"

"Linda," I asked. "Can you list your credentials for me again?"

"Well, I am former educator and principal. I raised a son with ADHD who went on to be a college graduate. I wrote a book about how to raise a child with ADHD. I guess that's it."

I could hear a gasp or two from other Celestial University students on the call. I bet they were thinking what I was thinking: *Who wouldn't want to work with you?*

I then assured my student that her ideal clients would clamber at the opportunity to work with her, but she had to believe in her abilities.

Linda feared rejection. Coupled with that, she had low self-worth, which happens when you rely on external feedback (praise and criticism) to validate your worth. I know I keep drilling this point, but it's an important one: *Loud Women must stop putting so much value on the opinion of others.* Instead, we must prioritize how we feel about ourselves from within. Our low self-worth is killing our Loud Women journey, and for many women, low self-worth provides a feeding ground for the Imposter Syndrome.

The Imposter Syndrome, also knowns as the Fraud Factor, plagues Loud Women everywhere. It's when you feel like you are not good enough compared to others. Here's how the Imposter Syndrome may show up for you:

- Feeling like you have less experience, education, or credentials than others in your industry
- Wondering "who do you think you are" giving out advice when your own business/life/relationship is a hot mess
- Second guessing why anyone would want to be attracted to you when they could be attracted to someone else prettier, smarter, thinner, wealthier, etc.

To get Loud, you must realize the "who do you think you are" message is your Ego. In fact, the Imposter Syndrome is really just another name for your Ego. All women, no matter their level of success, experience the Imposter Syndrome, too. It's common, normal, and, unfortunately, par for the course.

My friend Lynn, who is also an entrepreneur, experienced the Imposter Syndrome while attending a virtual alumni function. Lynn attended an Ivy League school, and the college hosted a Zoom call for alumni who are business owners. Lynn jumped on the call, but as soon as she did, the Imposter Syndrome struck.

It felt like most of Lynn's fellow alums owned six-and seven-figure businesses, or cool startups that may eventually sell for a lot of money. Lynn immediately felt "less than" because she was "just" an EFT practitioner, owning a one-woman practice. While her business is a success, she believed she paled in comparison to those of her peers.

Lynn knew the Imposter Syndrome was affecting her, and she decided to attend their second Zoom call with more confidence, convincing herself she *belonged* on that call, right next to those startups and million-dollar businesses. On the second call, she noticed the attendees came from different types of businesses and levels of success. It's interesting how her brain initially had focused on those "successful" ones with big profits and sexy exit plans. During that second session, she saw that she was one of many typical entrepreneurs, and she deserved to be there.

Guess what? After the second call, Lynn decided not to attend the next Zoom session, but not because she felt inferior to her alumni peers. She chose not to return because the energy of the group wasn't a good fit for her (as opposed to the other way around).

What happens if you cannot get a handle on your fears, low self-worth, and the Imposter Syndrome? Your Loud Woman journey can come to a screeching halt. In the case of Linda, the ADHD coach, that is exactly what happened. She could not get over her fear of rejection, her feelings of "less than," her reliance on what others thought—and she dropped out Celestial University. I worry that she closed her business, which saddens me to no end because many parents out there need her expertise.

Please do not let this happen to you. Work on your mindset so that when the Imposter Syndrome creeps up, you know how to put it to rest. Trust that you are here for a reason—and that you can do big things. You are a Loud Woman. Do not let the Imposter Syndrome tell you otherwise.

LOSING FRIENDS

My friend posted a racist remark on Facebook, and as I read her words, my mouth dropped. How could this woman—an educator, mother, and revered member of our community—have said such a thing?

I am an anti-racist, and I use my status as a white woman to educate other white women about how to be an anti-racist, too. Therefore, I decided to talk about my friend's comment, and how I felt about it, on my Facebook page and Instagram account. I did not mention my friend's name or identify her in any way, but I did quote her directly. I wasn't out to shame my friend, but I did want to teach a lesson: We need to stop belittling and insulting women, especially women of color.

My post went viral. I was pleased that so many women commented in support of what I was saying. The black women who commented did not mince words: My friend was a racist and her comment was unacceptable.

Within hours, my friend found out about my post and blocked me from social media. While I wasn't surprised, I had hoped she would read my words and see the error of her ways. When I realized she had blocked me, I was sad. We have been friends for many years, seeing her at our kids' sporting events, at the grocery store, even at stop lights. We helped each other with our aging parents and sweated together in concession stands.

Throughout our entire friendship, I knew she was conservative, and she knew I was liberal. And I prided myself in forming a friendship with someone despite different political ideologies. However, she became an ardent supporter of President Trump, and her language about Democrats and liberals became more hateful, referring to us dumb or baby killers or unable to see the truth. During the COVID-19 pandemic, she called anyone who wore masks and followed CDC guidelines "sheep."

As for racist comments, let's just say her post about this black woman was not the first time she made disparaging comments, but it was the first time she posted something so overtly racist. I am not a fan of hurting anyone, but what she said was despicable, and honestly, I should have addressed her directly.

This racist comment was the signal I needed to end this friendship. Even if she had not decided to block me on social media, it was time to say good-bye. Did I feel guilty? About some things, yes, but never about releasing a friendship with someone who refused to acknowledge her racism and learn to do better. In fact, what I mostly felt was relief. I had held back on posting my political beliefs on social media, for example, because I did not want to upset her. I felt like I was suppressing a huge part of myself by being friends with her. Now, with our friendship done, I felt more like my true self.

I wonder if she thinks I changed—from being someone who looked the other way, to someone who publicly and Loudly denounces what she feels is wrong. If my former friend thinks I have changed, she is right. I am Louder, and with that Loudness comes the permission slip to bless and release friendships that I have outgrown.

Your friends may not be on board with your Loud Woman journey, too. It sucks, but please don't let it stop you. You are here to change the world, remember?

The hard truth is this: As a Loud Woman, do not be afraid to outgrow friendships. In fact, it can be a beautiful process if you let it.

Very few of us have the same friends all our lives. Remember who you hung out with in kindergarten, sixth grade, and high school? Was it always the same group of friends, and are you still friends with them? Probably not. You may be connected on Facebook and have great memories, but chances are you probably outgrew each other a long time ago.

Friendships come and go.

Just like you outgrew those Guess jeans you wore in high school, some friendships are best left in the past. Bless and release relationships that no longer serve the Loud Woman you're becoming. It's okay to be sad about the loss of a friendship that has run its course, but it's not cool to allow friendships to become a yoke keeping you tethered to a post, forcing your growth to grind to a halt. It can be sad when it happens, but if you are clinging to friendships you have outgrown, you will not be as Loud as you need to be.

Loud Woman, your Loudness may trigger your friends. You may remind them that they are not living the lives they dreamed of. Perhaps they might be jealous of your positive changes. Or, your friends may be scared of losing your friendship. I hope your friendships can be salvaged with a heartfelt, vulnerable conversation, but sometimes they cannot. Know this is part of your journey, and it is okay. By releasing this outgrown friendship, you are making room for friendships that match your journey. You may find you're happier with like-minded friends!

As you continue on your Loud Woman journey, bask in the glow of your new friendships and the memories of the old. It really is a beautiful thing. Do not be afraid of losing a friend. Instead, focus on what will come next—more beautiful friendships, more fulfillment, more Loudness. It's what you deserve, Loud Woman.

47

RISKY

One of the riskiest things I have ever done was quit my corporate job after starting my business. My job paid well, had good benefits, and offered a lot of security. However, I was not flourishing in its stifling, political environment and did not like the inflexibility of my schedule. Running a business would allow me to work from home, which would save my family money on fuel, food, and child care. Plus, I knew I could make more money as an entrepreneur. Most importantly, I would have the freedom to set my own schedule.

It was a risk, though. Isn't it crazy to leave your secure job for the risky life of an entrepreneur? What if I sucked at marketing and sales, and did not get any clients? What if I hated working from home? What if someone sued me and took all my savings? As I decided whether or not to open a business, the "what ifs" flooded my brain, and I began to second guess my desire to be an entrepreneur.

I could sense the doubt tugging at the edges of my soul, and it frustrated me because I knew doubt clouded my judgement. I needed to do something more than sit and ruminate about my decision. What did I do? I opted to minimize risk.

Before launching my business, I planned out on paper what my business would look like, how I would market it, and how much I

would charge clients. With a written plan, I could visualize the possibilities. I opened my business while still working at my corporate job.
I decided that when I made the same amount of money in my business
as I was in my day job, I would quit my job—but not a moment
before. I hustled and got clients. Within four months, I was earning
more than my corporate job, and I turned in my notice.

You see how I worked through the risk? I planned, set goals,
worked hard, and eased my way to the risky part: quitting my job. I
am so glad I did because if I had not been brave enough to take this
risk, I would still be sitting in some cubicle, miserable, and probably
sick from the stress.

I quit my corporate job in 2011, and since that time, I have
sharpened my risk analysis skills (you have to as an entrepreneur),
which I use when determining whether or not to take a risk. Some
risks are worth it; others are not. If I can avoid spinning my wheels,
I will.

Society has taught women to avoid risks while encouraging men to
take risks all the time. What's up with that?

What's up with it is the patriarchal belief that women cannot
handle the consequences of a risk gone wrong. What if she gets hurt?
What if she gets upset? What if she is threatened?

Thankfully, a Loud Woman knows risks are part of her journey and
can handle anything that comes her way. She knows that to grow, she
must take risks.

Understanding that we must take risks is one thing, but taking the
risk is another. That's because our brains get involved. I am not saying
our brain's involvement is a bad thing; we certainly are smart and
capable. We need to prevent, though, Ego-based decisions and
Analysis Paralysis—both of which can happen when you decide
whether or not to take a risk.

If you are like me, you like to make level-headed decisions with a
gathering of facts and time to contemplate. However, when you do
that, your Ego and anxieties get time to talk you out of taking the risk.
And if you continue to overanalyze and decide to not take the risk, you
will never grow. That's not how a Loud Woman does it.

One of the questions I like to ask myself when analyzing a risk is, "What's the worst thing that could happen?"

In his book, *The Four-Hour Workweek*, Tim Ferriss talks about assigning a value to worst-case scenarios, like this: *On a scale of 1-10, what's the impact of taking the risk?* [32]

I like this idea, but I suggest taking it a step further by considering the *probability* of the worst-case scenario.

Let's face it: Our imaginations are amazing, and we can create stellar worst-case scenarios. However, the probability of a worst-case scenario may be slim to none, and it's important to identify this, too.

So, here's how I now assess a risk: I get out a sheet of paper, and at the top, I write: *What is the worst thing that could happen?* Then, I draw three columns:

- Column 1: Worst-Case Scenario
- Column 2: What's the probability it will happen (as a percentage)?
- Column 3: How bad would it be (1—hardly bad at all; 10—super bad)?

Then I let my imagination take over, documenting all the worst-case scenarios—no matter how small or improbable they might be. Once I am done, I can step back and determine how to proceed.

By evaluating the likelihood of my worst-case scenario, plus rating how "bad" it would be, I now assess if a risk is worth taking. This exercise calms my Ego down too.

I share this with you because I do not want you to talk yourself out of taking a risk. I also want you to take smart risks. If it helps, follow my method, or create your own. Either way, become comfortable with analyzing and taking risks because it is part of your Loud Woman Journey. Do not fear risks, Loud Woman. Instead, embrace them and watch how far you soar.

DISCOMFORT

Do one thing every day that scares you. Those small things that make us uncomfortable help us build courage to do the work we do.

— ELEANOR ROOSEVELT

48

WRITER

My Google drive is a graveyard of book drafts.

Some of the files are half-started stories and outlines, while others contain first drafts. After publishing my first book, *That First Client,* I knew I had tapped into a dream I had always squelched—to be a successful writer. After I released *That First Client* in 2016, I immediately started writing another book but abandoned it after a few months. Then I started a different book, and I abandoned it after the first draft. I wrote some more, trying different topics, and nothing felt right. I started another book and nearly finished the first draft, but decided to convert it to a six-month course.

With this record of incomplete books, I began to believe a writing career was not for me. I focused my creative energies elsewhere—on projects that I had more confidence in completing. Meanwhile, I kept reading other books written by women and felt a tug in my heart. This could be me if I just had the courage to stick with it.

You see what I was doing? I stayed in my comfort zone. Writing blog posts, creating courses, making videos, these are all things I can do in my sleep. I hid but felt powerless to change. Until I could no longer hide.

In the summer of 2020, I watched a Facebook Live announcement from Luvvie Ajayi Jones about her second book, *Professional Trouble-maker*. Being a huge admirer of Luvvie, I tuned in to learn more about her book. During the broadcast, Luvvie divulged that she experienced fears and resistance about writing her second book. Now, Luvvie is a *New York Times* bestselling author with a large community who adores her. It would seem that writing another book would be an easy, comfortable task for her, but she confessed it wasn't. I began to feel a little normal in my book-writing resistance.

Then, Luvvie posted this question: *What would you do if you weren't scared?*

I typed into the chat box, without a moment of hesitation, "Write a bestselling book that would change women's lives."

What?! What did I just type?! A bestselling book that could change women's lives?! Some kind of spirit possessed me and took control of my fingers because I would never dare type such a thing.

But I did. And as Luvvie scrolled through the responses in the Chat Box, she read mine out loud and declared, "Yes!"

Just like that, not only had I publicly declared I was writing a book, I received encouragement from someone I admire. In that moment, I also had something else: *My own blessing.* I was going to write a best-selling book that could change women's lives.

Woohoo! I'm doing this! I thought.

Another thought quickly followed, and it was louder, *Oh shit! What the hell am I doing?*

As soon as the "oh shit" seeped into my head, my Ego did what it does best: Fuel me with doubts to keep me in my comfort zone. And my Ego had its script ready: *Who do you think you are? You have tried this before, Jill, and failed miserably. Just look at your Google drive. Besides, who is going to listen to YOU? You are a fraud; you are not a Loud Woman. Hell, you are too scared to even finish, let alone publish, a book. What kind of Loud Woman is this? You'll get hurt, so you need to abandon this dream.*

Sure, my Ego presented a good case, but what my Ego did not count on was the emerging Loud Woman bubbling inside of me. She had been there all along, and she was tired of the back burner.

My emerging Loud Woman waited for my Ego to stop talking, and then she countered: *You are stepping out of your comfort zone. Yes, writing this book is scary but write it you must.*

Well, okay, then: I am writing a book. My emerging Loud Woman had spoken, and she was not putting up with my shit anymore.

I reflected on why I had abandoned my previous writing attempts. A lot of factors came into play, but one specifically concerned me: The discipline to write a lengthy book. My first book was short—less than 100 pages—and it did not take long to write. I knew my next book would be three times as long, and this fact daunted me. It almost made me want to abandon my book (again).

One of my superpowers is breaking a large project up into bite-size chunks. I can do it quickly in my head, determining the right increments to keep someone moving forward. I do this all the time for my Celestial University students. So, I stopped thinking about it as a book, per se, and I approached it like a project. When I made this pivot, the incremental steps dropped into my brain like dominos.

You see: Incremental steps are not just a logistical way to complete a project; they are steps out of your comfort zone. And when you take these baby steps, the project becomes surmountable.

My first step was to check out Scrivener, a software application used by fiction and non-fiction writers, including Luvvie, who enthusiastically recommended it during her Facebook Live. Scrivener had a 30-day free trial, so I downloaded it to check it out. I could see why writers loved it. For a visual person like me, it worked beautifully. I bought the license. First step done.

Then I gave myself permission to play, by creating a book section in Scrivener, complete with a basic outline and section placeholders. Awesome! Step two done.

I flew through those first two steps with confidence, and then I needed to take a larger step out of my comfort zone. It was time to write.

Even though I knew my book needed to be around 75,000 words, I didn't want to focus on the word count because it could scare me off. Instead, I committed to write fifteen minutes a day because it felt manageable and shifted my focus away from the word count. I fired up

Scrivener, set my times for fifteen minutes, and began writing. The time flew by, and lo and behold, I had turned out 500 words. Yay me! I was on my way!

The baby steps were working. What also worked was taking imperfect action. For example, I started writing my book without a thorough outline. In my past book-writing attempts, I always had a robust outline. This time, I started writing without one—just to get in the habit of writing those 15 minutes a day. Before I knew it, I had 5,000 words done.

Next, I knew I needed some accountability. While I had announced my intention to write a book during Luvvie's Facebook Live, I knew it would not be enough. So, I turned to Instagram Stories. Every day, I shared a photo of my total word count from Scrivener. Many of my Instagram followers messaged me to cheer me on. Now I was committed. If I publicly declared something and people responded positively, the project got done.

Finally, I took another step out of my comfort zone. I reached out to my friend Debby Kevin, who owns Highlander Press, to discuss the possibility of her company publishing my book. We had a great conversation, and at the end, Debby said, "I would love to publish your book." Holy crap! Now I had a publisher!

While I took these steps out of my comfort zone, my discomfort level shot through the roof. *Imposter Syndrome, present! Fear of Success, here, and I brought Fear of Failure with me!* This triad created a cacophony of noise in my head. Sometimes, they were loud and angry. Sometimes they were calm and reasonable. Always they wanted me to stop, asking the question: *Who do you think you are?*

It was hard to ignore these voices because they tapped into the most vulnerable parts of my soul, irritating me like a blister. I tried to tune them out, which only intensified their protests. I changed my approach, getting super quiet instead, and sure enough, a different voice emerged—my Loud Woman voice.

My Loud Woman voice was equally persistent, reminding me that women needed my wisdom. She kept saying, *just write the book, Jill. Keep going.* I decided to listen to her, and, imperfectly, I kept writing.

I am grateful for my Loud Woman's steady yet firm encouragement, because now, you are holding my book in your hands. My former comfort zone—the one mourning dead-in-the-dirt drafts—is a thing of the past. Looking back, I see all the milestones—all those baby steps. My Loud Woman voice helped me surpass each one.

There's a quote floating around the Internet that reads, "A comfort zone is a beautiful place, but nothing ever grows there." It's been attributed to a wide range of people from John Assaraf to Will Smith.

While I get the sentiment, I disagree that your comfort zone is "beautiful." Comfort zones are stifling, making you feel small and unimportant. One may argue that the *safety* of your comfort zone is beautiful, but that safety is a muzzle.

What is beautiful is the feeling you get when you take that tentative step out of your comfort zone, trusting you will land just fine. Yes, it's uncomfortable as hell as you pick your foot up to leave that safe space. But there's so much beauty in that moment, in that step, in what lies ahead.

IT'S UNCOMFORTABLE

L oud women get comfortable being uncomfortable. As much I believe this statement, I wanted to stamp my feet and whine, *but I hate being uncomfortable!*

Yes, discomfort feels, well, uncomfortable. But if you want to take up more space in the world and live your true and highest purpose, then yes, you must get comfortable being uncomfortable.

Let's talk about discomfort for a second. Specifically, why do we avoid feeling uncomfortable? Is it because it hurts? Maybe. Is it because discomfort brings up old wounds? Possibly. Is it because your Ego wants you to be small and safe? Oh yes.

Feeling uncomfortable conjures up the emotions we want to avoid the most: anxiety, fear, poor self-image, jealousy, and discontent.

However, avoiding these uncomfortable emotions are not the answer. Learning how to grow, in spite of them, is.

Have you ever been skydiving? I have not. And I hate to say "never," but truly, I never will. However, I am fascinated that people would jump out of a perfectly good airplane. The idea of skydiving makes me feel uncomfortable from head to toe.

I can only imagine the stories that pop into the skydiver's head: scenes of the parachute not working, the plane crashing, a bone-crushing landing, dropping into a tree...oh, my imagination would be on fire!

What must go through the skydiver's head when she's standing at the edge of the airplane! Again, I can only imagine, but I bet she's thinking: "Holy shit, what the hell am I doing?"

And then she jumps, falling to the earth, trusting her parachute will work and she will land safely on both feet.

And while she's floating, she might be thinking about how beautiful the earth is, how small we are in the grand scheme of things, how brave she is, how cold the air feels...

And when she lands, that skydiver must feel so proud, exhilarated, and unstoppable.

It's those final feelings, the ones when her feet hit the ground and her parachute drops to the earth, that pushes those previous uncomfortable feelings to the back seat.

That's why you must embrace the discomfort too. How else will you feel proud, exhilarated, and unstoppable?

In this section, we will tackle how to get out of your comfort zone, how to take imperfect action, reflect on when you have done hard things, learn tactics to help you survive the discomfort, and how to get more visible. By the end of this section, it's my hope that you will agree that discomfort is part of the journey. It's part of your growth. It's part of how you'll become a Loud Woman. And, you'll be okay with it.

COMFORT ZONES

L oud Women step out of their comfort zones. Notice I didn't say leap or jump. Loud Women just take one step, and often, it's a tiny one.

In her book, *13 Things Mentally Strong Women Do*, Amy Morin devotes a whole chapter to women and their comfort zones. She contends that people perform at their highest level when a little anxiety is involved. That means, to get out of your comfort zone, you have to balance between a little bit of anxiety (that baby step) and your widening comfort zone. She writes, "You have to keep moving to keep your stress at the right level."[33]

Once you take that initial step out of your comfort zone, keep taking more baby steps, or you risk complacency and lack of growth.

Let's not get ahead of ourselves, though. First, let's figure out how you can take that initial step.

Remember the story about my fear of flying? The first step out of my comfort zone was to book my tickets. To convince myself to purchase my tickets, I told myself it was just money, and if I couldn't physically get on the airplane, it was okay. I felt terrified, but these thoughts gave me enough courage to purchase my airfare. Once I cleared that hurdle, I contemplated my next step: Visualizing getting on the airplane.

So, what is your first step? It doesn't have to be a leap—just a baby step. Identify what it is and then take it. Before you attempt the second step, pause to celebrate your accomplishment. That first step is a game changer.

Want to know the secret to taking the first step? It's bravery.

Emotionally, you may never be ready to leave your comfort zone, and that's okay because you do not need your emotions in perfect order to take that baby step. All you need is courage. Or as Amy Morin says, "If you want to feel brave, you have to act brave. Change your behavior first and the emotions will follow."[34]

Look at the order here: Behavior then emotions. Action then feelings. When it comes to stepping out of your comfort zone, you cannot wait for your feelings to give you a thumbs up. It won't happen. You take action, trusting that the emotions will follow. And those emotions will prop you up for the next step out of your comfort zone.

One more thing: Look back at Amy Morin's quote about keeping stress at the right level. This means you will feel some stress—not the kind that makes your chest hurt or disturbs your sleep, but that little jolt of exhilaration, uncertainty, or curiosity. This little bit of stress is uncomfortable but not in a horrible way, like when you overextend your muscles after working out. It's uncomfortable, but not painful, and kind of feels good, too. That's the sweet spot you want to experience after exiting your comfort zone, time and time again.

51

IMPERFECT ACTION

Perfection surrounds us, Loud Woman. We see it on ads for make-up (perfect skin, eyes, smile, face, hair), on family TV (thin wife, fat husband), on Pinterest (converting Oreo cookies into a three-layer cake, hand-frosted, with a small swirl of homemade raspberry jam inside), and in Pottery Barn catalogs (entry tables with the perfect vignette of different-height candles, an empty birdcage, and the "Love Lives Here" hand-painted sign).

Career women are expected to do their jobs perfectly, look good while doing them, find time to exercise, have sex every night with their spouses, and be presidents of the PTA. For entrepreneurial women, we are expected to have perfect marketing, products, bodies, homes, and websites. And for stay-at-home moms, perfection oozes in every corner of their lives, from how the pantry is organized to the gluten-free, sugar-free, organic snacks for their kids.

It's ridiculous. Women—no matter their profession, marital status, or parenting style—all have the same thing in common: Do it perfectly and look perfect while doing it.

It's not the same for guys though. Just take a look at some of the more popular sitcoms through the years: *The King of Queens*, *Everybody Loves Raymond*, *According to Jim*, *The Honeymooners*, and *Modern Family*.

What do they all have in common? A perfect, thin, beautiful wife, paired with an overweight-but-he's-funny, often lazy, mostly sexist husband. Even cartoons like *The Flintstones* and dramas like *The Sopranos* have similar pairings. The women must look perfect. The guys? Not so much. [35]

Loud Woman, it's time to stop striving for perfection, no matter what you see on TV, billboards, and magazines. Perfection does not exist. It's unattainable, so let's stop spinning our wheels, trying to achieve something we cannot.

Thankfully, we are seeing more and more body diversity, messy homes, and imperfect meals in the media, but we have a long way to go.

While the media and entertainment industries catch up, here's something we can do: *Embrace imperfect action.*

Imperfect action is when you know you are doing a task imperfectly, but stepping forward anyway. Here's a little secret: once you get used to taking imperfect action, it's kind of exhilarating.

In 2015, I began recording videos to accompany my marketing blogs. What a hot mess. I held the camera wrong. I kept sweating. I sighed so heavily at the end of the video, it needed editing. Imperfect action! You know what though? I ripped that imperfect action band-aid off and kept going. I still make videos for my blog. None are perfect. I don't look perfect (acne, red scars, overweight, bad hair days); I don't sound perfect (hmm, umm, and you know); and sometimes the dog barks or the cats meow.

Here's how I look at it: If someone doesn't want to work with me because I have a pimple or say a few too "umms," she is not my ideal client. Bless and release.

Am I still plagued by perfection? Yes, of course! But where I've transformed is in the acceptance of this fact: *I will get a lot farther in my life if I take imperfect action.* And Loud Women, we have things to do.

Hell, this entire book is imperfect action. As I drafted this book, I wanted to rewrite and edit it all the time. However, I made a commitment: Write imperfectly and fix it up later. Imperfect action is how I got this book done.

Look around and see where you are striving for perfection. Then accept that you are chasing a pipe dream that will never come true because perfection does not exist. Then think about how you can take one imperfect step instead. For example, maybe you want the perfect body, but how about you imperfectly work toward getting your cholesterol to healthy level, or going down a dress size?

Your Inner Control Freak won't like it, and that's okay. Your Inner Control Freak is another guise donned by your Ego. Please do not take advice from your Ego. Get Louder by taking imperfect action.

52

ONCE HARD, NOW EASY

I was forty-five-years-old when I decided to do my first 5K. I signed up because I saw other women with race medals hanging in their office, and I wanted that too.

I also knew I would need to *train* for a 5K, and that would get me off my ass and help with my weight loss goals.

So, three months before the 5K event, I put on my sneakers and started walking. I could only go a mile before my shins screamed, and I had to stop.

Holy shit, this is really hard, I thought.

The next day, I tried again. I made it little over a mile before throwing in the towel. The sweat, the sore muscles, the heavy breathing returned in full force. I began to question my decision to participate in a 5K.

But I remembered that shiny medal I would get, and I kept putting one achy foot in front of the other.

Days turned into weeks, and I finally could walk a 5K. It resembled more of an ambling and took me about an hour, but I did it.

I then set a goal to complete a mile in sixteen minutes or less because I didn't want to be the last person across the finish line. This meant I had to pick up my pace.

I walked faster. My body protested in every way possible—sore feet, shin splints, achy back. My mind protested too, telling me doing a 5K was too hard and I ought to stop. Immediately, I ignored all those internal messages and kept training.

The day before the 5K, I picked up my race packet. I saw people of all fitness levels, sizes, and ages there and felt encouraged. I was almost at a sixteen-minute mile in my training, and I told myself in advance that it would be okay if I didn't hit it. *Just don't finish last*, I repeated, over and over again.

I gathered at the start line the next morning. I stared at the "real runners," smartly attired in their running shorts and old 5K race shirts. They gathered at the front of the start line, so I made my way to the back, where I assumed the slow pokes hung out.

As the race began, my body took over. I passed people who were walking slower than me. I would eye someone I wanted to get ahead of, and pumped my arms and legs until I did. For over three miles, I focused on passing the person in front of me.

I think I experienced adrenaline or maybe "the zone" that you hear from athletes. I shut out any mind or body protests, focusing on putting one foot in front of the other until I crossed the finish line.

As the volunteer draped the medal over my neck, I looked at my iPhone to see how long it took me to finish the 5K. My mile pace was less than sixteen minutes for the whole race. I almost cried in elation!

After that race, I was "addicted" to the feeling of accomplishment. I signed up for another 5K, then another, and eventually bumped up to 10Ks. Every race, I ignore the body and mind protests, and focused on getting past the person in front of me. Sometimes, I can't overtake someone, and that's okay.

When I look back at my first day of training, when one mile almost did me in, I smile. It was so hard when I first started. Now, it's so much easier. I can walk—even run—a mile without giving it much thought. I have shaved minutes off my pace. And when I join the start line, I no longer hang out in the back. You'll see me in the middle, right behind those real runners—but not far behind them. With each race, I got faster, stronger, and more confident.

Think back to a time when you had to do something that scared the shit out of you. Maybe it was trying out for a sports team, or asking someone out, or, like me, writing a book.

Your imagination concocted all sorts of "worst case scenarios." What if this happens? What if that happens?

But you set your sights on doing this task, and you did it despite your fear, and now you can do it all the time.

This phenomenon is called "once hard, now easy."

I first heard this phrase from my former business mentor, Fabienne Fredrickson. She explained that once we do the task we have been avoiding, it will be less scary. In fact, often by the second time, the task is easier to accomplish. By the third and fourth time, it's a piece of cake.

I definitely felt this as I overcame my fear of flying. It was so hard to get on that airplane the first time! For the flight home, though, I felt less nervous. And when I flew again, it was easier. Now, I can get on an airplane without giving it much thought.

Once hard, now easy.

All around you is evidence that you once did things that were hard. I bet you could think of an example right now.

Courage is contagious. Once you remember how brave you were in the past, it refills your Courage Tank and fuels you as you step out of your comfort zone.

So, when you are unsure about taking a step outside of your comfort zone, look back at when you did something despite the fear and discomfort. Remember how you felt before, during, and after you took that step. Those last feelings, the post-step ones, are where the magic is. Dwell in those emotions of elation, relief, pride, and happiness. Then put those emotions in your Courage Tank too.

Loud Woman, you can do this. Once hard, now easy.

53

LEAN IN

D iscomfort sucks. It can bring physical and emotional pain. It can cause insomnia. You may want to shovel chocolates in your mouth because discomfort sucks so much.

(Remind me again why we are signing up for discomfort?)

Here's what is important to know: You can get used to discomfort —to the point where it only bothers you a little bit.

I have never gotten a tattoo because I am not a fan of physical pain. When I have mentioned this to people with tattoos, most of them tell me, "It hurts at first but then you get used to the pain."

That's how it is with discomfort too. Yep, it is uncomfortable at first, but you will get used to it, and recognize it as part of the process.

I think the best way to handle discomfort is to call it out. Pull discomfort from your heart or head (or wherever you feel it in your body), hold it out in front of you, and say, "I see you, Discomfort!"

Once it's called out, you can figure out how to make yourself more comfortable. Often it helps to keep your "eye on the prize"—the end result you are after. "If I get through this speech, I will be brave enough to apply for paid speaking opportunities." "If she says yes to going out with me, I can focus on how much fun we will have together!"

Focusing on how you will feel on the other side is a great way to push through discomfort. Hand in hand, think about how you will feel once the discomfort passes—the feelings of elation, relief, accomplishment, and pride are motivators too (especially if you can anticipate those emotions during your period of discomfort). "I will be so relieved when this presentation is done!" "I will be so happy after my interview is over!" Feeling that relief and happiness *now* will not lessen those emotions after you reach your goal, either. In fact, it will intensify them.

At one point in my life, I weighed 250 pounds. When I looked in the mirror, though, I didn't see an overweight person. I saw myself. Then, I got professional pictures taken for my business, and when the proofs came back, I was horrified. I had so much fat in my face, it overshadowed my smile. It was then that I decided to go on a weight loss journey.

To help me succeed, I read a lot of books about weight loss. One book was *100 Days of Weight Loss* by Linda Spangle. She wrote about being motivated by your purpose, not the results. In other words, focus on why you are losing weight instead of what the scale's saying. Results can vary and fluctuate, and when you hook on to such moving targets, your motivation can waiver. However, when you hook on to your purpose, you will have the motivation you will always need.

That's the same for growth. Stay focused on *why* you want to grow. Your purpose will guide you through any discomfort. If you have to write your purpose on a Post-It note and stick it to your bathroom mirror, then do so. Always keep it top of mind. That's the best way to tolerate discomfort—and the best way to get comfortable feeling uncomfortable. Loud Woman, you can do this!

54

HIDING

Hound Dog Social Media was a dream come true—an opportunity to leave corporate, work from home, hang out with my dog, and get my kids out of before- and after-school care. No more commuting, no more corporate bullshit, no more wearing uncomfortable pants all day—just me and my mascot, Emma, and some amazing clients.

Running a social media marketing agency taught me a lot about social media, but it also showed me what I *truly* enjoyed doing: teaching. This became especially true when I worked with a client who wanted to establish herself as worldwide health expert. I wrote articles, optimized her YouTube channel, planned Facebook giveaways, edited her blog posts, created PowerPoint presentations, and gave her more ideas on how to grow her authority. I loved every minute. Not only did I enjoy teaching, I loved teaching emerging leaders how to market themselves. This type of marketing is called personal branding.

Back in 2013, personal branding was not a common term, and not too many people were experts in it. I saw this as an opportunity. I could help these entrepreneurs get more clients by marketing their expertise. So, in April 2013, I rebranded as Jill Celeste—Personal Branding Coach.

This business pivot rejuvenated me, and I poured myself in getting my name out there. Twice weekly blog posts, videos, robust social media, webinars, workbooks—I was on fire and increasing my visibility. As a result, I was attracting amazing clients, who loved learning how to use social media for personal branding.

One day, after holding a webinar, someone named Jamie Woods emailed me. He had received the webinar replay link and had a question about personal branding, which I happily answered. *Could this be a potential client?* I always loved post-webinar interaction, so I hoped to hear from Jamie again.

And I did! Jamie wrote back an even longer email. He asked some basic questions and attached a graphic for my opinion. While the questions seemed innocuous, something about the graphic put my "spidey senses" on alert. This graphic had an inspirational quote that was not inspiring. In fact, it looked like a parody, and I could not tell if Jamie was just bad at this or mocking inspirational quotes.

Listening to my intuition, I wrote Jamie back, ignoring his questions, and told him he would need to hire me if he had additional questions. When you request payment for advice, it tells you who is serious (or not). I figured I would not hear from him again.

The next day, I got another email from a man named Spike. Spike's email was professional and inquisitive, and had I not just dealt with Jamie, I would have been eager to respond to him right away. Now, though, I decided to research people who emailed me about my services. I wanted to know they were real—and serious—about improving their personal brand.

Spike was easy to find on Google because he is a sports commentator and the son of a legendary sports commentator in a large metropolitan area. Awesome! I was excited to learn that Spike was not only real, but he had a career that could benefit from a strong personal branding strategy.

I went to Spike's Twitter and scrolled through his various sports tweets. He had a few other tweets peppered in—mostly about his dad —and I began to feel excited about this potential client.

I don't know why I kept scrolling, maybe it was a nudge from The

Universe, but my mouse kept going and a tweet jumped out of his feed. Spike had tweeted that his brother was contacting personal branding coaches and messing with them. *Really?* I thought. I kept scrolling.

The next tweet contained a screen shot of another personal branding coach's tweet, and Spike's nasty commentary on what this person said. I could hear my pulse drumming in my ears. Wide-eyed, I kept scrolling, and found tweet after tweet of Spike and his brother badgering personal branding coaches. They would email these unsuspecting coaches to ask dumb questions, egging these good people to respond, which then prompted another email with more dumb questions. The brothers captured these dialogues and shared them on Twitter. They did not omit the coaches' names, and of course, they did not tag these experts so they could defend themselves.

Trapped now in a rabbit hole, I kept scrolling, looking for more evidence of these brothers' malicious behavior. On Spike's feed, I found the tweet I had feared the most—one about me. Spike took a screen shot of my autoresponder and made fun of the language in the email. Like with the other coaches, he didn't block out my name, and Spike's followers joined in the laughter.

In addition to being mad about how these brothers treated my colleagues, I was now humiliated. I wanted to hide and stop marketing immediately.

Tears welled up in my eyes, and I decided to stop looking at his Twitter feed. I had enough of the abuse.

Why were these guys trolling personal branding coaches? From what I could surmise, they did not believe in "personal branding." They considered it a faux marketing term made up by dumb people. How ironic, considering these young men lived a life of great privilege, thanks to their dad's personal brand.

I knew their type: self-centered, wealthy, entitled white guys who pick on others to elevate their self-worth. I had a decision to make: *Do I call them out, or do I ignore them?*

A huge part of me wanted to tell them off. They deserved it. They were malicious trolls who deserved to be knocked down a peg or two.

Another part of me, though, did not want to tangle with them. I knew it would be an energy suck, and I worried how it would appear to a potential client.

Plus, if I told these guys how mean they were, would they just screen shot my email and make fun of me more? Would it stop their trolling? Would they even care?

Well, they would only care because a woman outed them. Their behavior would continue, and their attacks on me would be more malicious.

I did not want more vicious attacks. I still had to respond to Spike's email, so I kept it short and simple. I told Spike I could not help him. Those were my exact words. It was the absolute truth: I could not help him with personal branding, and I could not help him be a nicer person. He and his brother were beyond my help, and I did not want to spend another second of my energy on them.

After I sent the email, I deleted Spike and his brother's alter ego, Jamie, from my email software. I turned on alerts to notify me when someone subscribed to my list so I could research each one. With this new process in place, I felt better. I wiped my hands clean of it all.

Now, at the time this happened, I was overweight and struggling with adult acne. I did not let my appearance stop me from making videos or taking selfies. Anyone who saw my content saw a smart woman with body fat and pimples.

Why am I mentioning this? Because the next morning, my email software notified me that someone had subscribed to my list late the night before. The person's name was "Eat Another Cheeseburger."

While I cannot prove it was Spike or his brother, I believe (to this day) it was one of them. It was a classic, pissed-off, white-guy-of-privilege move. *If she's unmoved by my prior malicious acts, then let's start fat shaming her. That'll teach her to try to outsmart me!*

I did not care that someone called me fat because I was fat. What bothered me was they thought they could get away with the fat shaming. It was unacceptable behavior.

I went on Twitter and headed over to the brother's account. Sure enough, he had tweeted another malicious attack on a personal branding coach (not me), and this time, I "liked" his tweet. I showed my hand, letting him know that Jill Celeste—Personal Branding Coach was on to him. It was a simple act, but I knew it would get his attention. I waited for his next move.

Sure enough, Brother Troll tweeted me back, asking if I enjoyed his correspondence. I tweeted back, "It was hilarious." Just like that—no explanation point, no emoji, no LOL! Just a sarcastic comment I knew he would get.

A day or two later, I blocked Spike and his brother's Twitter because I kept scouring it for comments about me, and I knew this was unhealthy. I did not care anymore. They could say what they wanted. I was out of fucks and had no more time to spend on mean-spirited trolls. I could not—would not—allow them to destroy my mindset. I was not going to run and hide. Instead, I discarded them like the trash they were.

As a marketing teacher for female entrepreneurs, I talk a lot about getting more visible through marketing. I encourage my students to "stop hiding" and get out there in big ways to reach their ideal clients. In fact, I teach them to replace the words to Olivia Newton-John's song, *Let's Get Physical*, to "Let's Get Visible!"

For women, getting visible can be scary because it is uncomfortable. It's like going out in the world naked. However, the more a woman gets visible, the easier it becomes.

If you don't own a business, you obviously do not need to get visible to gain clients. But you are not off the "let's get visible" hook because many women hide in many different ways:

- Not advocating for causes that are important to them
- Not getting paid what they are worth
- Not sticking up for those who are vulnerable, discriminated against, or need a helping hand
- Not campaigning for a political candidate they support
- Not going for that promotion
- Not seeking a higher degree
- Not writing a book

- Not making that speech
- Saying "yes" when they mean "no"
- Not writing your politicians about things they want changed
- Not defending other women and people of color against sexist, racist, and xenophobic attacks, especially on social media
- Not blowing the whistle on something wrong at work
- Staying in relationships with people who do not value them
- Not bouncing back after failures
- Avoiding conflict—big and small

You see: Visibility isn't just for entrepreneurs. It's for every Loud Woman. We cannot hide anymore. We cannot rely on others to use their voices. We must get out there with our Loud Woman Voice, and tell people how we feel and why.

Will this be comfortable? Probably not. That's how you know it is the right thing to do. Remember when I said fear is a signal? If you're scared shitless about something, it's a sign from The Universe to proceed.

In the next chapter, I will talk about using your social media platforms for social good. For now, though, think about what you would like to get visible about. What's worth getting uncomfortable? You can do it because that's what Loud Women do.

55

SOCIAL GOOD

Y ou have a platform. It consists of your social media accounts and followers. If you're an entrepreneur, it also includes your email list and networking colleagues.

A platform is just a fancy word for the people who surround you and the ways you reach them.

What if every woman in the world used her platform for social good? What if she used her Facebook, LinkedIn and email to share a message that makes our world a better place?

Wow, what a tsunami of feminine power that would be!

In her book, *Untamed*, Glennon Doyle talks about how people become passionate about things. It's often the result of a heartbreak. "Every world changer's work begins with a broken heart." [36]

It's through this heartbreak that purposes are found and communities are forged. While it may seem overwhelming, when you got that Divine Tap, you will feel unfulfilled, even unsettled, until you agree to light the torch. It's the ultimate act of bravery for many women, and to me, it's one of the cornerstones of being a Loud Woman.

We see this all around us. A heartbroken mom formed MADD after her thirteen-year-old daughter was killed by a drunk driver while walking to a church carnival. Never Again started after the high school shooting in Parkland, Florida. And then there's Greta Thunberg whose righteous anger about environmental issues has inspired whole countries to act.

You also see it in Chanel Miller. Chanel is the sexual assault victim known as Emily Doe, who was assaulted behind a dumpster at Stanford University. In 2020, Chanel revealed her identity and released her memoir, *Know My Name*. Chanel could have gone on with her life, but instead used her platform as Emily Doe—now Chanel Miller—to share her message. And her message was a big one, illuminating how sexual assault victims are treated unfairly by the court system and outsiders.

As an entrepreneur, I have a platform too. Truthfully, for many years, I avoided using it for social good. While I am passionate about many issues, I thought it would be better to keep social issues and my business stuff separate. I was wrong.

I learned I was wrong after reading a letter called "I Need to Talk to Spiritual White Women About White Supremacy" by Layla Saad. She penned this letter after the white nationalist march in Charlottesville, Virginia, in 2017. The white nationalists descended upon a small protest at the monument for Robert E. Lee. They beat a black protester with poles. After the incident, President Donald Trump assured us there were "good people on both sides."

Like many people around the world, what happened in Charlottesville sickened and disgusted me. And so was Layla Saad. But what sickened her *more* was the silence of spiritual white women, many of whom have a large social media presence.

Her letter began with an account about Charlottesville and the racism she experienced in England. It was hard to read. In fact, I would start to read it and have to stop. And as if Layla was reading my mind, she wrote:

I'm wondering how you're feeling right now as you are reading this letter Uncomfortable? Outraged? Helpless? Ashamed? Wanting to do everything you can to stop this and yet feeling like you have no idea what you can do or say? I hear you. It's overwhelming and confusing and triggering as hell.[37]

She went on to explain how this discomfort and fear was more so for black people, and that when events like Charlottesville occur, it reminds them how far they need to go to achieve equality.

"This right far surpasses your white shame, white fragility, and your white privilege of staying silent," she declared.

She then addressed white female entrepreneurs who stayed silent about what happened in Charlottesville. Our silence was not helping; in fact, our silence perpetuated the problem.

Gutted, I saw how wrong I had been to stay silent. As a white female entrepreneur, sending only "love and light" as a remedy to these terrible issues was wrong. My role was to speak up, to use my white privilege to illuminate the problems in our world, and to inspire change.

That's when I made a dramatic shift in my social media marketing. I scheduled a ninety-minute Facebook Live, making sure to promote it so people would attend. During this Facebook Live, I read parts of Layla's letter—the hard parts my community needed to hear. I openly denounced racism. I told my community they would no longer find me silent. Finally, I told people to unlike my page immediately if they agreed with President Trump that there were good people on both sides.

After this Facebook Live, I became more vocal about racism, always condemning it and trying to inspire my community to look deep within themselves. I also became more vocal about better awareness and policies for victims of sexual assault. I even created a course called Celestial Changemakers that assembled female entrepreneurs who wanted to use their platforms for social good. Through my own course, I wrote a manifesto and shifted some aspects of my business.

And while I was more vocal, I also learned to talk less and listen more to my sisters of color. When they said something was racist, I believed them without argument. When they said something was a result of white privilege, I did not get defensive. I kept my mouth shut and my ears open.

So, what's my business social media marketing look like now? I unapologetically talk about human rights issues. I use examples of

Loud Women, including politicians, to empower my followers to get Loud in their lives. And when another Loud Woman uses her platform for social good, I support her by making sure to comment.

Is it perfect? No. Is it scary? Yes. Am I afraid to make a mistake? All the time. But all of these fears are better than silence.

Luvvie Ajayi Jones in her book, *I'm Judging You*, reminds us that our positions are powerful ones and to use our voices to make real change in the world, even though it's almost paralyzing to do. Why? "Sometimes we feel pressure and self-imposed expectation that when we do something it needs to be big and perfect. That renders us useless..." [38]

We do not have to advocate perfectly. We need to accept that mistakes will be made, and these mistakes are lessons to help us improve our advocacy. It's okay to be wrong *and let other people see it.* It's okay to apologize. All of this okay: Staying silent is not.

If you are feeling uncomfortable about speaking up about something on your platform, that's a signal to speak up. Chances are others are uncomfortable too, and that's exactly why you need to use your voice. If you have something to say about racism, say it. Same goes with women's rights, how immigrants are treated, the welfare of children, climate change, and the myriad of other causes that need Loud Woman Voices.

"When our voices shake, that's when the words need to be heard the most," Luvvie assures her readers. It's hard to speak the truth on important things, but we cannot be silent.

One more thing: If your audience —whether it is your business followers or the people who are friends with you on Facebook—do not like what you're saying, it's okay. If they decide to unfriend or unfollow you, that's okay too. They are not your people.

Our world is at a crossroads. If we all stay silent and afraid, our world will take the dark path at this crossroads. However, if Loud Women like you and me raise our shaky voices and talk about what's wrong in the world, we will take the illuminated path. And that illuminated path will lead to positive change.

TRUST

Trust yourself. Create the kind of self that you will be happy to live with all your life. Make the most of yourself by fanning the tiny, inner sparks of possibility into flames of achievement.

— GOLDA MEIR

56

CYST

The second blue line wasn't even faint. My pregnancy test showcased those two blue lines like it was auditioning for a spot on the Las Vegas strip. I was pregnant!

Unlike many women who wanted to play it safe and wait to tell people, I couldn't dial my parents' phone number fast enough. By the end of the evening, my parents, sister, brother, in-laws, and best friend all knew I was having a baby.

As with most first pregnancies what happened to my body felt novel yet nerve-wracking. Was I feeling the right amount of morning sickness? Was I peeing too much? Shouldn't I be showing? I wore out the pages of *What to Expect When You're Expecting*, looking up every little flutter, sensation, cramp, and jab (not to mention the weird poop). I was always assured—either by my book or by other moms—that what I felt was a normal part of pregnancy. Innately, I knew they were right, but there's nothing like a pregnancy to bring out the jitters.

I was about three months pregnant when I felt a dull pain on my left side. Nothing jabbing or excruciating—just a little *boop* that shocked me more than hurt me. Knowing that pregnancy brings interesting sensations, I made a mental note of it and went on with my day. Daily, the pain reminded me it was still there, sometimes more acutely. I decided to call the nurse at my doctor's office, and she asked that I come in. Relieved, I headed over to their office, knowing I was about to be reassured that everything was okay.

The nurse listened to my symptoms, and, suspecting a urinary tract infection, handed me a urine collection cup. Despite the test results coming back normal, the nurse said, "If it walks like a duck, and quacks like a duck, it's a duck!" Then she handed me a prescription for antibiotics.

As I stood in line at the pharmacy, I felt skeptical that my "duck" was a urinary tract infection. At the same time, I felt assured that it *could* be, which also meant it's treatable.

Knowing antibiotics take a few days to do their magic, I patiently tolerated the pain and tried to keep my mind on other things. My husband and I discussed baby names and our plan to move to a bigger apartment. In the back of my mind, though, I still felt like something was amiss.

By Sunday morning, the pain intensified. The antibiotics hadn't brought any relief. I called the doctor's after-hours hotline. A nurse midwife returned my call. I had interrupted her church service, and I will never forget the joyous noise in the background.

After hearing my concerns, she assured me I was okay. She told me, "Sometimes pains are in your head." I hung up, feeling defeated. No one was taking me seriously. Self-doubt settled in. Was I being a hypochondriac? Was I making up this pain in my head? Was I just being overly anxious? I remember laying around all day in bed—miserable in body and heart.

The next morning, I knew I had to advocate for myself more. I mustered up my inner Loud Woman, called the doctor's office, and secured an appointment for later that day. I practiced my spiel.

Dr. Van Zandt burst into the exam room, sat on a stool, and held my hand, as I explained the pain I felt. In addition to my symptoms, I told her about my conversation with the nurse midwife and how I felt brushed aside. I also revealed that *intuitively* I knew something was wrong. She squeezed my hand and proceeded to give me a full exam.

As she felt my belly, she looked at me with kind eyes and enormous confidence, "You have a cyst on your ovary. I can feel it."

My eyes widened until they looked like two saucers. *A cyst?* She explained how some women develop cysts right before or during their pregnancy, and as the baby grows, it becomes painful. The cyst usually resolved itself, but she wanted to monitor it. She scheduled an ultrasound and told me exactly what to pay attention to. Finally, I felt better. While I was not thrilled to have a cyst, I had been heard, and my instincts were right. Now we could address the problem.

A few days later, I laid on the table in the ultrasound room and saw my baby for the first time. What a wiggle monster! I also saw the cyst, and I watched as the ultrasound technician measured it. She took the information over to Dr. Van Zandt, who reported back that I would get another ultrasound in four weeks to check out things.

As I waited for my second ultrasound, the baby and pain were my constant companions. I chose not to focus on the intensifying pain, instead focusing on the first flutters of my baby. Four weeks later, I was back in the ultrasound room, and I learned two things: the baby was a boy (yay!), and my cyst had grown significantly and rapidly larger (oh shit!).

Dr. Van Zandt wanted a better view of the cyst, so she referred me to a high-risk obstetrician with a high-powered ultrasound machine. Laying in another ultrasound room, I awaited the verdict. The doctor held my hand as she confirmed my suspicions: I did not have a typical ovarian cyst. In fact, mine was bigger than my baby. She recommended surgery to remove the cyst, urging me to speak to my obstetrician right away.

I cannot even describe the fear that gripped me as I tried to process this news. I went from believing I had a benign, harmless ovarian cyst, to a mystery mass that was growing by the day—*and* the doctors were not sure what it was. Cancer? Dermoid cyst? In my head, it all added up to bad news. I sat in my car, my hands white-knuckling the steering wheel, not sure if I should go back to work or go home. I chose the latter.

I no sooner got home from the specialist appointment when my phone rang. It was my doctor's office, wanting to schedule a consult to discuss the next steps. While I was grateful for how swift things were moving, the speed intensified my worry. *They are moving quickly because they are concerned,* I thought.

The next day, I sat in the office of Dr. Young. I brought my mom, a retired nurse, with me. Here were the scenarios Dr. Young spelled out for me:

Option 1: Have major abdominal surgery to remove the mass. This would require, more than likely, the removal of my left ovary. If anything went wrong during the surgery, which was a likely risk, I would have to decide on whether or not to abort my son. If the baby survived the surgery, I would inevitably go into labor, requiring medication to ward off the premature delivery. If the medicine did not work, my child would be born very prematurely, and his survival rate was poor.

Option 2: Leave things alone. This also meant we would not know what was growing inside of me. If it was cancer, they could address it after my pregnancy. If the cyst was something else, and it ruptured, I would probably need an abortion because the toxicity of the ruptured mass would hurt (or kill) my unborn child. This route also was riskier for me, as I could die too.

Those were my options. I closed my eyes to absorb the news. My mom asked more questions, and her voice became more distant as I went inside of myself. I was tuning in like a radio dial to pick up internal advice on how to proceed. A voice boomed back: *Have the surgery. Everything will be okay.*

On September 2, 1999, I sat in a hospital bed with my husband by my side. I was calm, surprisingly enough. As the transporter wheeled me away, my husband cried. I can't imagine how scared he must have felt seeing his pregnant wife taken away for risky surgery.

I never had surgery before, and all of my senses were on high alert. The transporter took me to the pre-operative area. The machines beeped and everything seemed so white, almost blinding as I took in the sterile environment.

I felt a warmth, though, from the nurse who approached me. She wore a surgical mask, so I couldn't see if she was smiling, but her eyes smiled. This nurse told me her job was to sit with me during the entire procedure, and that if I needed anything, she would help. You see, I would be awake during the surgery. I couldn't have general anesthesia because it could hurt the baby. Knowing she was there to help me alleviated some of my anxiety.

In addition to my companion nurse, I met the nurse midwife whose job it was to hold my son—in utero—above my body as the doctor worked on removing the mass. Then she would gently place my child back into my body. I said a prayer, right then and there, asking God to guide her hands. She would be holding the most precious cargo ever.

During the surgery, I felt a lot of tugging, and my heart rate went up as anxiety kicked in. The amazing surgical team all rooted for my son and me. Once the mass was removed, Dr. Young stapled me up twenty-nine times, and I think we all said a prayer. *Please, God, let this baby live.*

I'm not going to sugar coat my recovery. It was hell. I was doped up on morphine and took magnesium sulfate to ward off pre-term labor. The "mag" (as it was called) did a number on me. I struggled to inhale or exhale, like I had to tell my brain and lungs how to work. I thought I was dying. My mom, who had driven forty-five minutes one way every day to sit with me, rubbed my hand, reassuring me my breathlessness was just the medicine and everything would be okay. I trusted my mom's opinion and began to repeat in my head the mantra I had been repeating this whole pregnancy: *Everything was going be okay.*

After three miserable days, I began to feel better. The labor stopped. My son had a strong heart rate, and I could feel him kicking. By day five, I was released to go home, and spent the rest of my pregnancy on bed rest.

My son, born on December 27, 1999, came into this world with a loud scream and a red face. I would be screaming too if I endured what he had. I had worked very hard to bring this child into the world, and I thanked God for this miracle.

As I sit here, typing this story twenty-one years later, I think about the scar I now sport on my stomach. It looks like a jagged silver zipper. When I see it, I am reminded of how I listened to myself, how I advocated for myself and my child, and how yes, everything had turned out okay. My scar constantly reminds me of what happens when I trust myself, listen to my intuition, and turn inward to listen to my body.

If you listen, you will make the right decision, and you will hear, like I did: *Everything will be okay.*

SELF-TRUST

Okay, you're all set now. You're going to call the program, Social Media 180, right?" I asked.

"Yeah, I am so excited," my client replied. "Thank you for helping me find a name for this program and what it entails!"

"I am excited for you, too! You can do this," I said, hoping my client would take this momentum and start marketing this brand-new program we co-designed for her business.

About three hours later, my client posted on Facebook: "What do you all think of the name, Social Media 180? Do you think it's a good name for a program I want to teach?"

Face palm. *Didn't she just decide on Social Media 180 as her program name?*

In this post, my client didn't explain the program and how it could help business owners do a "180" on their social media marketing. As a result, her friends all poo-pooed the name. They offered her other ones instead. Her simple question resulted in getting more ideas than she needed.

Guess what happened next? She didn't feel comfortable with Social Media 180 anymore, and she didn't like any of her friends' suggestions. So, she put the program on the back burner. Now, she didn't have a program to sell, which affected her income, and her clients did not receive this critical training. This was the opposite of a win-win.

And it's what happens when you don't trust yourself.

Do you trust yourself?

At the surface, you may think: *Of course, I trust myself!* I hope this is true, but based on my experience, most women do not trust themselves.

Here's why: We are surrounded by other people's feedback and opinions—from the people we live and work with to those on social media. If you are hanging on to every word of criticism and praise you receive, you don't trust yourself. In addition, you may listen to others before trusting yourself to decide or form your own opinion.

This mistrust can manifest in constant information seeking, such as when you must acquire a lot of knowledge before deciding—to the point where you are over-learning as a procrastination tactic. Professionally, you always feel the need to get another degree, license, or credential. Personally, it could mean hours spent researching on the Internet, often sifting through conflicting information.

When you do not trust yourself, you also crowdsource your decisions. You ask your friends and family for their input, and you often reach out to social media, too. That means you are making decisions based on feedback from people who do not know you well, or worse, complete strangers.

When you do not trust yourself, you are in a constant flux. Like an indecisive squirrel, you dart around in a panic. You feel unsettled and will procrastinate on your decision until you can research it (more) and/or crowdsource.

You often regret your decisions. This is a natural extension of indecision and not listening to yourself. Others are not as vested in your decisions, yet you listen to them because you are unsure. So, when you get bad advice, it's no skin off their back, but you are unhappy as hell. It's not the way to live.

It's time to trust yourself, Loud Woman. In this chapter, we break down why we stopped listening to ourselves (yes, we used to listen to ourselves!), and learn more about your intuition, confident decision-making, and trusting you are the best expert of your life.

My hope is that you feel empowered to trust yourself, gain confidence, crowdsource less, and feel like you can make *your own* decisions. Let's get started.

INTUITION

Several years ago, I began working with an intuitive mentor, Nicole Meltzer. Nicole teaches women how to tap back into their intuition, despite years of ignoring it. When I signed up to work with Nicole, I did so because I wanted to hear *her guidance*. Nicole is highly intuitive and can channel, and I yearned for this divine guidance. Nicole had other plans, though. She wanted to rebuild my own intuitive muscle so I would not have to rely on her, or anyone else, to get intuitive guidance.

In our sessions, she started with asking for what advice I sought, and then led me into a meditation. Nicole's meditations are guided, and she would ask me to note what I would see on my journey. For example, she would say, "There's an object next to you on the ground by your feet. Pick it up. What is it?"

When we came out of the meditation, Nicole asked what objects I saw. At first, she would interpret them for me, but after some time, she started asking other questions like, *what does that object mean to you? Why do you think this object appeared in your meditation?*

When Nicole first asked these questions, I thought she needed additional information from me. Instead, she was showing me I did not need to rely on her guidance because my intuition was there, ready to help, if only I would tap in and listen.

Through our sessions, I began to interpret the meditations with more confidence. I realized I didn't need a third party to help me interpret what my intuition was telling me. Thanks to Nicole, I now tap into my intuition at a moment's notice. I know how it feels in my body (I get a tingle on my scalp). More importantly, I trust it.

We all have intuition. You may call it your sixth sense, gut feeling, or instinct. Whatever its name, your intuition is real, and it is there to help you. As a Loud Woman, never ignore it.

Intuition comes from the Latin root, "intueri," which means "consider," and Medieval Latin "intuitio," which means "a looking at, immediate cognition." As these ancient origins show, your intuition is part of your body, and something you look at and consider.

So many times, though, we do not.

As young children, we used our intuition all the time. Crawling, walking, sucking, gurgling—these are all examples of our intuition at work. As we got older, other sources, such as our parents, siblings, teachers, and friends, began to influence us. Our intuition still guided us, though. Think about how toddlers play: without prejudice and so much exploring. It is amazing to watch little ones play, guided by their intuition.

At some point, though, we stop listening to our intuition. How does this happen? Sometime in our past, a person of influence told us we were wrong. Now, I am not talking about a correction. I am talking about a person who you loved, admired, or respected gutted you in some way, whether by strong criticism, admonishment, or bullying. This traumatic event taught you to stop listening to your intuition because it resulted in hurt feelings. And just like that, you began to ignore your intuition.

Brené Brown discovered this when researching childhood shame. In her book, *Daring Greatly*, Brené writes, "One reason that I'm confident that shame exists in schools is simply because eighty-five percent of the men and women we interviewed for the shame research could recall a school incident from their childhood that was so shaming that it changed how they thought of themselves as learners." [39]

I wonder what percentage of this eighty-five percent wished they listened to their intuition, instead of the feedback from an influential person at school. I bet it's a lot.

Can you remember when this happened to you? You may remember a specific incident, or recall a series of them—ones that chipped away at your intuition until you surrendered and stopped listening.

I do not remember a specific incident, but I can recall times when influential people belittled me to the point where I ignored my intuition. When I reflect on these incidents, I think about how I must have looked receiving their criticism—like a drooping flower whose pedals were falling off, one by one.

You see, even at a young age, we learn to hook on to others' feedback. We begin to crave praise and try to avoid criticism to boost our self-worth. So, when someone told us our intuition was wrong, we listened and believed. This continues until we learn to untangle from the need to be approved by others and plug back into what our intuition is telling us. Wow, if I had listened to my intuition instead of someone else, I would have saved myself a lot of heartbreak.

Often, Loud Women mistake intuition for their Ego. Here's how you can tell the difference: Your Ego plays full blast in your head. And if you ask yourself why you feel a certain way, you can list *all* the reasons.

Your intuition, though, sweeps in, creating sensations like a "feeling" in your gut. If you try to explain it, you cannot put a finger on why you feel this way. That's because your intuition does not come from the logical, explainable part of yourself, but it is there, nevertheless.

When you listen to your intuition, you are leaning into your self-trust. In fact, "going with your gut" is the highest form of self-trust, which is why you need to embrace your intuition more.

Thankfully, it is never too late to tap back into your intuition as I learned by working with Nicole. That is because your intuition is always there. It takes practice, though, because we need to rewire our mindset and trust ourselves again. It can be done, though.

Loud Woman, could you listen to your intuition more and your Ego less? It is your intuition that will guide you on your Loud Woman Journey. And she will do so beautifully, as long as you listen.

You may need someone to help you, and that is okay. I know some women undergo hypnosis to recall the time when they began to mistrust their intuition so they can heal from it. Others, like me, employ the help of an intuitive mentor, who will teach you to listen to your intuition again. And others can do the work themselves by meditating, journaling, and dreamwork. This is your journey. Do what feels right to you.

I will say it again: Listening to your intuition is the ultimate form of self-trust. It is also a crucial part of your Loud Woman Journey. If you can ignore the advice from your Ego, disregard the guidance from external sources, and tap into your intuition instead, your confidence will soar. You will take the bold steps you need on this journey. Often, when women say, "There is something missing from my life," what is missing is their willingness to listen to their intuition—and then trust what she's saying to you.

No more, Loud Woman. Listen. Trust. Everything you need is inside of you. Your intuition was put there for a reason—just like your heart and lungs. You did it as child, and you can do it again. The fulfillment, bravery, and confidence you want has been with you all along—you just need to tap into it.

59

BOTTLE FEEDING

My husband and I sat on the floor of the hospital classroom, eager to learn about how to take care of our soon-to-be-born son. I was nervous about taking care of a newborn. Bathing with an umbilical cord? Diaper changes? Swaddling the baby? These questions, and more, danced in my mind.

As we got situated, the instructor asked us who was breastfeeding and who was bottle feeding so she could give us the right supplies.

"I'm bottle feeding," I said, so she handed us a baby doll, bottle, burp cloth, and diapers. I looked around and noticed I was the only mom who chose bottle feeding. Thankfully, the other moms were respectful and did not shame me for this decision.

Unfortunately, the same could not be said about the instructor. While talking about breastfeeding preschoolers, one pregnant mom joked, "That kid's going to be a serial killer!"

The instructor quickly retorted, "No, that's the bottle-fed kids."

The other moms' laughs erupted around me. I clutched the baby doll to my chest; the earth caved in around me. I had not even birthed my son, and I already felt "less than." I promised myself—right then and there—that I would never tell anyone about my choice to bottle feed. The shame was unbearable.

Here's the thing: I should not have to lie. I made this decision after careful, thorough research and soul searching. I educated myself about bottle- and breastfeeding and weighed the options against what I knew would work best for me. I was healing from life-threatening surgery performed in the middle of my pregnancy, which set off subsequent health issues. My body felt depleted and needed a rest. I was raised on baby formula, as were countless others of my generation, and we are all turned out fine. I knew the best decision for me (and my son) would be to bottle feed. It would bring less stress to an already stressful time.

I also knew I would be a better mom by *not* breastfeeding. Some would say I was being selfish, and they are right. A mom is allowed to make selfish decisions.

Twenty-one years later, as I look at my healthy, adjusted, productive young adult sons, I have *no regrets* about bottle feeding. I am glad I trusted myself and listened to my instincts. Mothering is hard enough without discounting what your intuition is telling you.

Which brings me to this question: Who knows what is absolutely best for you?

It's not your spouse, or your parents, or your best friend. It's not your boss or therapist either.

It's you.

You are your best expert.

Somewhere along the way, you may have lost sight of this. As kids, we relied on our parents or other authority figures to know what's best for us. We were young and learning about the world, and these authority figures helped us find our way (albeit imperfectly).

However, we instinctively knew as children what was best for us. We often suppressed this in deference to these authority figures' advice. In the process, we suppressed our innate expertise. We did it because we were not confident in our abilities, or to be polite, or because it seemed easier.

What happens, though, when you abandon your role as your Best Expert?

You do not live your life to the fullest. You feel an inner discontent that can manifest into other things, such as addictions, depression, and unhealthy relationships.

As your Best Expert, your decisions may not be popular with those who want to influence you, and that's okay. As long as you made the decision knowing what's best for you, proceed with confidence. Try to remember that someone else's opinion of you is none of your business.

Think about the times when you listened to someone else's advice and ignored your own. How did that work out for you?

I bet it did not work out in the best way possible *for you*. That's what happens when you ignore your instincts, intuition, and gut, and let an external source decide what is best for you.

You are your best expert, Loud Woman.

Trust your intuition. Build your self-belief. You know what is best for you. You truly do.

60

FAITH

As a teenager, I had unwavering faith that I would attend an out-of-state college. I had to finance my education and heading out of state meant higher tuition. Nevertheless, I wanted out of Florida, so I requested catalogs from out-of-state colleges. My parents were troopers, schlepping me to Georgia and Alabama so I could visit campuses. It was on one of these trips that I visited Wesleyan College in Macon, Georgia, and knew exactly where I wanted to attend college.

Wesleyan, a small, private, all-women's college, had expensive tuition, room, and board. Despite the price tag, I could visualize myself there. I attended a scholarship weekend where I could win a full scholarship, thinking *This is it! This is my chance!*

About two months later, I checked the mail and saw an envelope with Wesleyan's logo. I ripped open the envelope, right there by the mailbox, unable to wait another second to learn what scholarship I had won.

But the letter bore other news. I hadn't won the full scholarship—or any scholarship. I was gutted. Despite this, I refused to give up on my dream. As my peers made their college commitments, I held on and stayed in faith. Somehow, I knew I would get to Wesleyan College, even if I did not know how.

Several weeks later, after high school graduation practice, the phone rang. It was the financial aid office at Wesleyan. They pieced together enough scholarships and loans to pay for my tuition, room, and board. I cried when I heard these words! My persistence and faith had paid off. That fall, I'd be at Wesleyan!

When I graduated cum laude from Wesleyan four years later, I had a mile-long list of student leadership positions and awards. I repeated this journey to get to graduate school—always staying in faith—and that time, I won a full scholarship to get my master's degree.

To be so young and to have stayed in such faith, even when I saw no evidence that my dream would come true, amazes me to this day. When I feel my faith flickering, I remember the eighteen-year-old Jill who refused to give up. I remember manifesting scholarships to attend the colleges of my choice and staying in faith even when the journey brought me detours and speed bumps. That memory fuels me on days when I feel like giving up.

The dictionary defines faith as "complete trust or confidence in someone or something." Faith could mean having trust in yourself. Faith could also mean knowing God has your back. It also could mean you do not know if it is you or God (or both), but you believe in this power with all your might. Your definition of faith may be different than another Loud Woman's definition. All of this is okay. What is most important is that you stay in faith and never give up on your Loud Woman Journey.

Why is it so hard for us to stay in faith? I like to think about the quote from *Miracle on 34ᵗʰ Street*, when Kris Kringle wisely said, "Faith is believing in things when common sense tells us not to."

Humans love "common sense." We have been hearing about common sense since we were little girls:

- *It's common sense that girls cannot play football.*
- *It's common sense for girls to wear dresses to church.*
- *It's common sense that a quiet girl is a good girl.*

Is there a "Common Sense Rule Book" somewhere where the rules of common sense are written down? No, of course not. That's because common sense is a societal construct to keep women quiet, small, and safe (not to mention what it does to men). And our Egos love to latch on to the "common sense" message to explain why we shouldn't do something.

So, when we rely on common sense, we do not embark on our Loud Woman Journey. We lose faith and quit our dreams. I say to hell with common sense. Have faith instead.

Another reason why we lose faith is because we do not know *where* to step forward. Martin Luther King, Jr. once said, "Faith is taking the first step even when you don't see the whole staircase."

What happens, though, when that first step is not in our view? What if that first step is clouded over? That's when we tap into faith even more. If you listen to faith, it will tell you it is okay, that faith has your back, and that you will not fall. Faith will tell you to take that first step, even if you cannot see where you are stepping.

That is hard as hell, right? It is uncomfortable to step on to a staircase you cannot even see.

Remember when I talked about stepping out of our comfort zones? How we should take a baby step instead of a flying leap? That's how we approach these often-hidden staircases. Take a baby step. You will feel more comfortable if you drag your toe out there and feel your way around. Once you feel more certain, you can take another baby step, and then another. Increments are you friend, and if taking incremental steps helps you step out on to a staircase you cannot see, then so be it.

And if your Ego keeps telling you to stop and turn around, respond with this: *Thank you for your advice, but I am going to step on to this hidden staircase.* As you say this to your Ego, you are saying this to yourself, too. You may have to repeat it to both of you, and that's okay. Just keep going!

What happens when you do not stay in faith? You give up. Worse, you are not living your life to its fullest expression. Now you have replaced discomfort with regret and regret always makes you feel like shit.

When you are losing faith, look back at times when you stayed in faith and were so glad you did. Like me, I bet you have the ultimate "stay in faith" story. If you need to, write it down so you can read it on days when faith starts to slip away. This memory of staying in faith is the proof your common sense is looking for. If you did it once, you can stay in faith again.

We need Loud Women across the world to take that first step, even if the staircase is hidden, even if it feels scary and uncomfortable. Push past your discomfort by remembering that you believe in yourself. Drown out common sense and replace that message with ones of faith. Trust yourself. Trust your decisions. Trust that the journey will pay off.

Loud Woman, in case you need to hear it, I believe in you. I can see you pushing through fear and discomfort, allowing faith to seep into your life. I see you taking that step. Maybe it's only a centimeter forward, but you are taking it. Hold this vision with me. Trust yourself. Believe in your dreams. Stay in faith even when you cannot see how to proceed. You got this.

SUPPORT

I call upon women to raise each other up, to make each other's welfare a priority, and to never shame a woman for the choices she makes.

— FREIDA PINTO

INVESTIGATOR

I needed to get away, so when my business mentor announced she was coming to Orlando (only two hours away from me), I jumped at the chance to go. I decided to stay an extra night after the conference ended so I could decompress and enjoy some additional "me" time.

You see: I had never traveled without my family. Leaving them for four days scared me a little, but I needed to do this. For all of us, I wanted to prove I could leave and the house would still be standing when I got back.

Before I left, I emailed all of my sons' teachers to let them know I was going on a business trip. I warned them that my boys may be out of sorts because we were not often separated, and I asked that they be gentle with my kids if they acted out at school. I included the guidance counselor in my notification, figuring better to be safe than sorry.

The business conference was exactly what I needed, and left feeling refreshed and energized about my business. When I got home, I eagerly awaited my boys' arrival because I missed them so much.

I greeted each of my sons as he came through the door, languishing in their hugs and school news. I noticed my oldest son had worn an old shirt to school and chuckled to myself. He wouldn't have made it out the door in that shirt if I was home, but I loved that he made his own clothing decisions.

This same son mentioned he got in trouble at school that day, but he insisted it was not a big deal because he did not receive any detentions or suspensions. I made a mental note to investigate this further, but at that time I just wanted to enjoy our reunion.

A little while later, a loud knock echoed through our house—not completely surprising considering how many kids live in our neighborhood. When I opened our front door, a woman with a police badge stood on my porch.

"Hi, I'm Officer Russo from Pasco County Child Protective Services. Are you Mrs. Celeste?"

Stunned, I could only nod, grasping the side of my front door for support.

"We have a complaint from the school that we need to investigate. Can I come in?"

Wait, what? A child protective officer was at my door? This had to be a mistake.

The confusion must have been written all over my face because the investigator firmly, but assuredly, followed up, "I need to come in and ask you some questions—that is all."

I opened my door and led her to my dining room.

What transpired next was the child protection officer interviewing both of my kids, plus my husband and me. She asked about my son's school and social life, his discipline problems, and what help I got for him. I even had to show her that I had running water, and she inspected his room. It was the most undignified, humiliating experience of my life.

Thankfully, I am an organized mom, and I was able to show the investigator my son's educational plan created by the school, copies of his last psychological exam, all of his report cards, proof he was undergoing additional psych testing by the school, and, most importantly, a copy of the email I sent his teachers and guidance counselor just days before.

The investigator let me know the school lodged the complaint because they thought we were neglecting Anthony based on a hole in his shirt and long nails, plus his repeated discipline issues.

Before she left, she asked for the names of my son's pediatrician, psychiatrist, and psychologist. The investigator indicated she would speak to all of my son's teachers, a member of administration, plus three references that I needed to provide. Embarrassed, I thought of three people who would not judge me too much for being investigated for child neglect.

I walked the investigator to the door, and as I bid her good-bye, I turned around to found my sons staring at me. I wanted to lose it—to cry and pound my fists—but I needed to reassure them first. I hugged them and told them to put their shoes on because we were going out to dinner.

I rushed to the bathroom, claiming I needed to freshen up. As soon as I closed the door, I crumbled to the bathroom floor. Wracked with guilt, I told myself I would never leave my boys again. I persecuted myself for being so selfish—to take four days away—because if I had not, a child protection officer wouldn't have shown up at my door.

I knew my kids and husband were waiting, so I only let out one big, ugly sob, composed myself and washed my face. It was time to restore some normalcy, despite the fears that weighed me down. *What if they take away my kids?*

A few days later, the investigator called to ask some clarifying questions and passed along an update. My son's clinical team reported they had no concerns about our care of him, and my other son's school said the same. However, the conversations with the assistant principal (who I suspected lodged the complaint) and some of Anthony's teachers painted a different picture of me.

Specifically, the teachers (all female) remarked how I didn't display emotion when they shared things about what my son did at school. This left them wondering if I cared about my son's behavior. Then, the assistant principal (a female) indicated my son was in the office a lot because he had authority issues (he has oppositional defiance disorder, as indicated in his educational plan), and he "sometimes" came to school with holes in his shirt, and unkept hair and nails.

In sum, these female teachers and administrator all said the same thing: *I was negligent.* Side note: These educators are moms and had been teaching for years.

After she gave me this information, the investigator dropped this bomb, "The school is not on your side, but the school has been very negligent."

She said the school should have done psychological testing on my son sooner because it was apparent he was on the autism spectrum. The school also dropped the ball on including an appropriate discipline section on his educational plan.

She speculated they were trying to build a case to expel my son, or to make me so angry that I would withdraw him from the school.

The investigator said that my son took up a lot of resources (ones he has a legal right to), and she felt like they just did not want him at the school.

She needed to continue her investigation, but she finished our call with some amazing advice on how to handle my kid, additional records I needed to keep, and assurances she had seen countless boys like my son, and they all turned out all okay.

My investigator had turned into my ally, my advocate.

Several weeks later, I called her to ask about the status of the case. She told me the case was closed. She concluded that my husband and I did not neglect our children and commended us for doing a great job. She offered even more information about my son's schooling, rights, and needed documents. I remember her saying, "I just wanted you to have the best information so you can navigate these waters without interference from my department again."

What started out as a horrible situation turned into one of valuable support, thanks to this investigator. I suspect she knew from our initial interviews that I was not negligent, but she left no stone unturned because she sensed that things could get better. Who needed to improve, ironically enough, was the school.

I also felt better about taking that four-day business trip. The guilt dissipated as I realized I didn't do anything wrong.

This is what happens when a Loud Woman supports another Loud

Woman. You lift, help, give advice, gather all of the information, don't wield accusations until you get all the facts, and do the job God put you on this Earth to do.

Before this experience, I had a negative view about Child Protection Services. The media reports how they are overworked and uncaring. While I have no doubt they are overworked, this investigator cared deeply about my son and his future.

As for the female teachers and administration, at the time, I feigned politeness but wanted to tear their eyes out. Upon my son's request, I did not move him to another team of teachers or remove him from the school. His friends—the few he had—were in his classes, and I was not about to add more trauma to his life.

Trust me: I have a soft spot for educators. Why this small group of educators had it out for Anthony is something I don't know. My guess is he made their jobs harder—and their jobs were hard enough.

I can forgive them for that. We are all humans, doing the best we can.

What I wish I could tell them now is that I would have loved their support—instead of their judgement. They shamed me in the worst way as a parent. I would have asked that they put themselves in my shoes, especially as moms. I would have said:

Think about being a conscientious, openly communicative, get-all-the-resources-for-my-kid parent, like I was, and then have to defend yourself to a member of law enforcement. Think about the days spent worrying about your children being taken away, blaming yourself for going away, and overanalyzing every parenting decision you ever made.

Parenting is a hard job, and those teachers knew this. I think they were steeped in their own views, probably feeding off each other after hard days, and that was the result.

Here's another thing I would have said, "I forgive you." Because that's what Loud Women do.

STAND UP

The eight of us clinked glasses and cheered our much-needed Girls Night Out. We curled our hair and put on our best blouses, and we escaped the demands of motherhood, marriage, and life.

Despite being away from the demands of our personal lives though, our conversations were always about our personal life, especially parenting. We all had kids about the same age, and we swapped stories to seek advice and lift each other up. It was therapeutic to know you are not alone on this journey of motherhood.

I didn't realize when the night started that this would be my last Girls Night Out—at least with this group of women. Why? Because what was supposed to be a night of support turned into a night of gossip.

You see, one mother, Elizabeth, could not attend our Girls Night Out. And my friends took advantage of her absence to criticize how she was raising her kids.

"Her daughter is out of control," one friend announced as she stirred her drink.

"Agreed," several friends murmured, looking at each other with confirming nods.

It's true that Elizabeth had a precocious little girl and Elizabeth struggled disciplining her.

"It's like she doesn't care," another friend bemoaned. "She just lets Ashley do whatever she wants! And that mouth on her…"

"I'd slap her to the next week."

Round and round the conversation went. I watched in dismay. Is this what happened when you don't go out with friends? They pick you apart for how you're raising your kid?

I have a difficult child too. And I wondered, *What the fuck do they say about me when I'm not around?*

At no time did any of these friends (including me, regrettably) stick up for Elizabeth or offer ideas on how to support her. Instead, it felt like these friends were cutting down Elizabeth's parenting style to elevate their own—just to make themselves feel better.

On the ride home, I shared my thoughts with my friend, Vicky.

"You know, I felt sad that everyone was picking on Elizabeth. We don't really know what it's like to be her or to raise Ashley. Maybe she's doing the best she can."

"You're probably right," my friend remarked with a shrug.

"I think I should have said something," I continued. "Anthony gives me a run for my money. Mothering is hard enough without people talking about you behind your back."

My friend shrugged again.

As I pulled into my driveway that night, I decided to never go out with these friends for a Girls Night Out again. I couldn't be part of conversations where we tore apart how other women raised their kids. I just couldn't.

A surefire way to stop the rise of Loud Women is for women to not support each other. It always boggles my mind to see or hear a woman berate another woman about her attire, mothering skills, or how much she weighs. As members of a patriarchal society where sexism permeates, it's essential to help each other. We encounter enough road-blocks without us adding to it.

Unfortunately, women tend to not stick up for each other, as evidenced by how women talk about and to each other in conference rooms, social media, and PTA meetings.

Why do we do this? A lot of it comes down to competition. For example, some women feel like they need to step on their female co-workers to get ahead. When it comes to mothering, it can feel like we are competing for "best mom ever," even though no such reward exists.

Additionally, many women have low self-esteem, so to elevate it, they point out other women's flaws. Having a bad hair day? Well, at least it's not as bad as hers. Pants too tight? At least I am not 100 pounds overweight like her.

As you get Louder, you may be ridiculed and shamed. It sucks. It may make you want to hide and be quieter, but please don't. Instead, pour your energy into something else: Supporting other Loud Women.

The good news is that as you wave your Loud Woman Freak Flag, you will attract other Loud Women. Now it will be your job to support all these Loud Women even if:

- Her weakness is your strength;
- Her method for getting Louder is different than yours;
- She's showing her competitive side; and
- You may not agree with everything she is doing.

These differences may make you uncomfortable or activate your Inner Judge, but try not to go there. A rising tide lifts all boats—no matter what kind of boat it is. We need every Loud Woman united to cause this tide swell—or we will end up with no Loud Women.

We cannot have a world without Loud Women. We have been in a Loud Man world for too long, and look where it has brought us: war, climate change, corruption, and poverty. If you are like me and want to reduce or eradicate these calamities, we need to be Louder.

Most of this book has focused on your individual efforts to be

Louder, but we cannot ignore this important fact: *Loud Woman is a movement.* It is a collective. It will only work if women band together in their Loudness. To accomplish this, not only do we have to work on our individual Loudness, we must support other women on their Loud Woman Journey.

In this section, we will talk about "rising tides" as well as why women compete with each other. We will also focus on helping other women reach their potential and how to support a woman who is different than you. Also, I will discuss (quite frankly) how fellow white women need to support women of color.

Supporting other Loud Women, on paper, feels right. However, when we are in the trenches, it can be hard to do. We have odds stacked against us. We are still working on our own Loudness, imperfectly and messily, and to find the bandwidth to support other Loud Women can be hard. It can trigger fears of not being liked, or of being criticized, and or being ignored.

That's okay. This whole process is a hot mess at times. Forgive yourself when you screw up and vow to do better. That's the best we can do. Trust me: Our best is *way better* than our current state.

63

SOMETHING ABOUT HER

H ave you ever met a Loud Woman and not like her—but you cannot figure out why?

Maybe it is the way she walks or that knowing smile she wears. Maybe it is the confidence in her voice or the way she dresses. Whatever the reason, when you look at her, you get a knee-jerk reaction not to like her.

Glennon Doyle experienced this as she watched a confident soccer player during her daughter's game. The young player walked with a swagger and gave off an air that being a good soccer player was so easy for her. Glennon, in her shock, realized she was hating on a twelve-year-old. Why do we do this? Glennon explains:

> It's because our training is kicking in through our subconscious. Strong, happy, confident girls and women are breaking our culture's implicit rule that girls should be self-doubting, reserved, timid, and apologetic. Girls who are bold enough to break these rules *irk* us. Their brazen defiance and refusal to follow directions make us want to put them back into their cage.[40]

It saddens me to admit that I have been guilty of disliking Loud Women in the past, and I still grapple with it today. As Glennon said, my subconscious kicked in—to the point that I could not tell you *specifically* why a particular Loud Woman rubbed me the wrong way. Or as Glennon put it, "I don't know, I can't explain it—it's just something about her. I just don't like her. I can't put my finger on why."[41]

Thanks to Glennon's wisdom, I now know why I cannot put my finger on this disliking and distrust. I am reaching for an age-old story. That "something about her" message is a byproduct of my societal conditioning that Loud Women are obnoxious and cannot be trusted. While I hope this initial knee-jerk reaction goes away over time, at least now I recognize it and can work my way through it.

The "something about her" phenomenon is what happened to Senator Elizabeth Warren when she ran for U.S. president in 2020. For sure, Senator Warren was more than qualified to become the President of the United States. She was a cabinet member, U.S. senator, and law professor, spending years teaching and learning about consumer economics. She is smart, wrote plans about taxing the super wealthy and paying for childcare, and had a down-home approachability despite her elite resume.

So why didn't Senator Warren win the Democratic nomination? Sexism absolutely played a part. This showed up as a question of "likeability" and "electability." Senator Warren ran for president during a time when voters wanted someone who could beat President Donald Trump. Many voters liked Senator Warren, but they did not think she could beat him. So, they voted for someone else.

And why couldn't she beat Donald Trump? For many voters, it came down to "there's something about her." They would reference her voice, pant suits, hair, even her devotion to her dog. But these were just distractions, hiding the real reason: *Americans were uncomfortable with Senator Warren because she was a Loud Woman.* Confident, funny, and outspoken, she was not afraid to push her viewpoint. Unlike many women, she did not *give up* on pushing her viewpoint either. This relentlessness showed when she attempted to read Coretta Scott King's letter on the Senate floor during Attorney General Jeff Sessions' nomination. Her Loud Woman move left many people thinking: *I just don't like her and I am not sure why.*

But we know why, don't we? Senator Warren did not exhibit any traits that a woman is supposed to have. Confidence, knowledge, *and* likes beer? A plan for everything? It threw people off and made them uncomfortable, just like that twelve-year-old soccer player did to Glennon.

So, who did the Democratic voters choose instead? Something they were used to—Joe Biden, who is like most of the presidents who served before him (old, male, and white).

Senator Elizabeth Warren and other female candidates also face the shitty truth that they are held to a higher standard than their male counterparts. Male politicians can cheat on their wives, pay hush money for their one-night stands, avoid military service, and say something sexist—and they are forgiven and elected. *Oh, boys will be boys,* they say. Indeed.

A female candidate, on the other hand, must be squeaky clean. Knowledgeable but not cocky. Confident but humble. Straightforward but polite. And she must have all these traits while having every hair in place and perfectly shaped eyebrows. It's no wonder women do not want to run for office.

But what would happen if we as Loud Women stopped holding other Loud Women to these impossibly high standards? What if we supported a Loud Woman no matter her confidence or the tone of her voice? What if we applauded women with knowledge and plans? What if we supported Loud Women who walked with a swagger and wore what she wanted?

What if we, as Loud Women, saw the *there's something about her* excuse for exactly what it is—a signal that we are succumbing to societal conditioning? What if we said instead, "Yes, there goes a Loud Woman!"? And because of her swagger, confidence, plans, and knowledge, what if we supported her enthusiastically and unabashedly?

If we do this, Loud Woman, we would create a world where Loud Women are in places where we should be, from youth soccer fields to the White House (and everywhere in between). As Ruth Bader Ginsberg once declared, "Women belong in all places where decisions are being made. It shouldn't be that women are the exception."

Then, women can rise with confidence, knowing other women are not tearing them down. The world would be in a such a wonderful place with smart, feminine leadership shining from every corner.

Loud Woman, there *is* something about her. That something is her Loudness, and it is a wonderful thing.

When you see a Loud Woman and you feel that societal conditioning creep up, push it down—*then raise her up*. Show your support. She may not be getting Loud the same way as you, but she is getting Loud—and that deserves your support. With enough practice, you will change that subconscious wiring of instant distrust to Loud Women who are breaking society's rules. It may be messy at first, but please stay the course.

Our world needs less "there's something about her and I don't like it" and more "there's something about her and it's wonderful!" Will you embrace this with me?

64

COMPETITION

I was in that awkward place between graduating from college and starting my graduate program. Awkward because I didn't know what to do with myself for nine months. Knowing I needed to save money, I moved home to get a "real" job (something that paid more than minimum wage.) Pretty quickly, a local department store chain hired me as a manager in training.

This job suited my nomadic spirit because it allowed me to travel around Florida to open up new stores. I enjoyed the blank canvas—setting up the fixtures, displaying the merchandise, and training the new employees.

The first store I opened was in Indian Rocks Beach, Florida, which was a long commute to an unknown area. I felt excited. Even though I had zero intentions on getting promoted, I still wanted to put my best foot forward. I arrived at the store, met the team, and quickly got to work.

Things were going great! In addition to setting up the sales floor, I spent a lot of time training the new supervisors: three women from three different walks of life who now had the most responsibility for the store. I learned about their lives and struggles. Admittedly, after leaving my idyllic, supportive all-women's college, I was a bit wide-eyed about what these women's lives were like. I enjoyed our conversations and probably asked them more questions than they asked me.

It was around the fifth day that I noticed a shift with two of these women. After a long day of moving racks of clothing, I exited the store and saw them chatting by the curb. I wished them a good night, and I was greeted with a snarl from one and a forced smile from the other.

Their reactions took me aback. I was not sure what had transpired, and in my naivety, I assumed I had interrupted a confidential conversation, and they didn't appreciate being interrupted.

I am thankful for my naivety that day because if I had known the truth, I would have ruminated on it for days—and my self-esteem would have been taken a nosedive.

You see: My employer and colleagues assumed I had taken the manager-in-training position to learn retail management and become a manager of my own store. But for me, this job was a pitstop along the way to graduate school. I didn't feel I could disclose my graduate school plans to anyone because I needed this job and feared I'd be fired if they knew my bigger vision. So, I played the part and worked hard because I wanted to make a good impression—even if I did not desire a promotion.

One of these supervisors, Cyndi, thought I was angling to be the manager at her store. Cyndi wanted to be the manager instead. In her head, the only thing standing between her and the manager's position was me.

Once this thought took hold, Cyndi did what a lot of women do—she saw me as competition. And, like many women, she felt the only way to handle her "competitor" was to bulldoze me.

Months later, I learned how this supervisor had attempted to smear my reputation. First, she spoke about me to every manager and director that entered her store that week (which was a lot because new stores attract a lot of management). Cyndi told them that she did not see why I was such a "big deal," and how I was not ready to be a manager. Then, she spoke to her fellow supervisors to rally their support, telling them I would be a "lousy manager" and how she was a better fit for the job.

When my area manager told me about Cyndi's sabotage, I was floored. I had never been treated like that by anyone. I could not wrap my head around why she would bad mouth me like this. Did she really think destroying me would help her?

It was comical, really, because this supervisor got so upset about me for no reason—I didn't want the job! I just wanted to make some money and move back to Georgia for grad school. She barked up the wrong tree in so many ways.

Despite the comedy of the situation, I was devastated and deeply hurt. I had befriended this woman and listened to her life story. I trained her to the best of my ability. I liked her and thought she liked me too. I never dreamed she would go behind my back and say such mean-spirited things. I felt betrayed.

My twenty-two-year-old self learned a valuable lesson from Cyndi: *Some women will trample on you on the way to the top.*

Why do women do this? Why do we sabotage other women in an attempt to elevate ourselves? Two big reasons pop up: a scarcity mindset and trying to get ahead in a patriarchal structure.

Let's first look at scarcity mindset. This is when you believe things are in a limited supply, such as money, jobs, clients, relationships, and time. When you have a scarcity mindset, you believe there's only so much and you must compete to get your share. When you have a scarcity mindset at work, for example, you believe *this is my only shot.* Cyndi had a scarcity mindset because she believed this manager's position was her only shot at getting promoted, which led her to make fear-based, wrong decisions.

The opposite of a scarcity mindset is an abundance mindset. This is when you believe there is plenty for everyone. An abundance mindset takes the pressure off of you. You realize "competition" does not exist because there is plenty of money, promotions, love, and time for everyone.

On your journey as a Loud Women, your Ego may set off the "competitor alarm" about a fellow Loud Woman. That's old programming. No woman is your competitor—no matter how Loud she is. Sink into an abundance mindset instead, remembering there's enough for everyone.

Hand in hand with a scarcity mindset, women are also trying to get ahead in a world dominated by men. Look at what happens in the workplace. Few women get promoted to management and C-level positions; a woman feels like she is competing *with everyone* to get ahead. If there's a way to knock down others who might get promoted too, many women will seize it. It's not just a competitive drive, though, that's driving these women's mindsets. Low self-worth is in charge. When you add low self-worth to a scarcity mindset, a woman may decide to elevate her chances by trampling the other women on a similar path.

It may be a while before women get equal access to promotions. For now, though, a woman can work on her mindset by understanding there's an abundance of things and that there is no competition. That way, women won't trample on each other on the way to the top.

For sure, trampling and badmouthing are the exact opposite actions you should do as a Loud Woman. Abandon the scarcity mindset, first and foremost, so you understand there is plenty for everyone. Increase your self-worth so you know you are worthy of a promotion, or more money, or a better relationship. You can attain what you desire without stepping on anyone along the way. Understand there are no competitors on your journey, that what transpires for you is meant to be, and that if you don't get this one, something else even better will open up.

And in the workplace, Loud Women support other Loud Women because they know how hard it is for a woman to get promoted. And so, if you are passed up for a promotion and another woman gets it, celebrate her. You know how hard this is. That's the ultimate way of showing your support.

Loud Women, there are no competitors. There is plenty for you and every other Loud Woman out there. Embrace this knowledge and support each other. When you do, more Loud Women will emerge— and this world will change for the better.

65

WHITE WOMEN

B reonna Taylor's killers got away with murder. The three police officers who killed Breonna were not charged. Adding insult to injury, only one officer, Brett Hankison, was charged with wanton endangerment for shooting into apartments adjacent to Breonna's. Those walls got more justice than Breonna did. It sickens me to this day.

When Kentucky's attorney general announced what the charges were (or more accurately, what they were not), many black women expressed their anger on social media. These black voices united in an unmistakable, sad truth: *Any one of them could have been Breonna.*

It does not matter if these black women made their readers uncomfortable by expressing the truth and their feelings. It does not matter if they cussed. It does not matter if they were confrontational.

What does matter is their righteous rage. They earned every right to be pissed. They, unapologetically, should use their social media to voice their outrage. That's what Loud Women do.

However, white women began to feel uncomfortable with the black women's disgust, calling on black women to be less divisive and more peaceful. Luvvie Ajayi Jones got messages like this, and here's what she reminded all of us, "I am a Black woman first and your weak ass 'let's be nice' stance is trash and you are part of the problem and you are not welcome here."[42]

White women: We must do a better job in supporting our black sisters and other women of color. Period. End of story. Let's set this intention together, right now, by repeating after me: *As a white woman, I will do a better job helping women of color.*

Once you have set the intention, it's time to abandon perfection, roll up your sleeves, and get to work. We have no guide book here. We are learning as we go. But learn and go we must. People's lives are at stake, so time is of the essence.

Please know I am learning too. Imperfect, messy, and fearful, I am navigating my role as a White Loud Woman, learning from my mistakes and the mistakes of fellow white women.

I want to share with you what I have learned so far. Know it is not a complete list of how to do a better job as a white woman, but it is a starting point.

#1: WHITE WOMEN MUST LISTEN.

First, white women must listen. And I mean *really listen*—not listen for a pause in the conversation so we can talk. The Loudest thing we can do is to be quiet and listen with our hearts.

#2: WHITE WOMEN MUST EDUCATE THEMSELVES.

What we learned in school is a white-washed version of our history. White women must be curious and seek out education that explains what really happened to people of color, especially in the United States. Thankfully, modern scholarship has provided us many books, movies, magazine articles, and TV shows that will help you learn more about being a person of color in the U.S. As a starting point, check out my list of books in the "Recommended Reading" section.

A word of caution: Remember that all women of color do not have the same viewpoint on any specific issue. Often, in our quest to learn, we will ask a woman of color to give their feedback as if she represents the whole race. Instead of asking, "what do women of color think of..." ask this question: "What do you think of...?"

#3: WHITE WOMEN MUST BELIEVE.

We must believe people of color. If they say something is racist, it's racist (honestly, wouldn't they know what is racist more so than us?). If they say something is unjust, it's unjust. If they say something is white privilege, it's white privilege. Trust what they are telling you— without trying to justify or defend it. This includes non-visible minorities, such as white Jewish women. If she says something is anti-Semitic, believe her.

#4: APOLOGIZE WITHOUT EXPLANATION.

If you make a mistake, say you're sorry without explanation. We explain because we want to show our good intentions and assure women of color that we are not bad people. That's an effort to make *us* more comfortable, and it's irrelevant. Sometimes you will say the wrong thing; sometimes you will mistakenly stay quiet. It's inevitable because it is a messy process. Just remember that mistakes will occur, and when they do, say, "I'm sincerely sorry. I won't do it again."

#5: DO NOT BE AFRAID TO MAKE A MISTAKE.

Society does not easily forgive women for their mistakes. This is an extension of a patriarchal society, and it's wrong. The only way to combat it is to be okay with making mistakes. If it helps, replace "mistake" with "lesson." Women of color do not have time for us to sit around and try to be perfect on our anti-racism journeys. When we try to be perfect, it's an extension of white privilege because we do not feel the sense of urgency. Trust me: It's urgent. Let's accept that we will make mistakes, say sorry when we do, and take the lesson with us.

#6: BE GRATEFUL FOR THE EMOTIONAL LABOR OF WOMEN OF COLOR.

Show gratitude for the emotional labor spent by women of color who are correcting us, sharing their experiences, and educating us about racism. I cannot imagine how exhausting this is, especially because they are often saying the same things over and over again. When a woman of color shares her experiences or tells you how to do better, thank her. She does not have to do it, so it's a kindness when she does. If it's possible, compensate her for her time. This is an important gesture and goes a long way toward healing.

#7: USE YOUR VOICE TO SUPPORT WOMEN OF COLOR.

Use your voice to support women of color. Even better, amplify their voices with your voice. Remember how I talked about using your social media platform for social good? You can do this by sharing the work, wisdom, and talents of women of color. Because of systemic racism, women of color face obstacles in getting their messages out. We can support by lending our platforms.

#8: CALL OUT WHITE WOMEN FOR THEIR RACIST ACTS.

It's our job as white women to call out other white women for their racist acts. Remember, most women of color are not believed, so we must step in. You may feel uncomfortable doing this, especially when the white woman is your friend or relative. But you cannot let racism go unchecked, even if it comes from Grandma's mouth.

#9: DISCOMFORT IS PART OF OUR JOURNEY.

Finally, understand that being uncomfortable is part of the journey. With discomfort comes change. Think how uncomfortable it is for a woman of color to face racism every day. Your discomfort is minuscule compared to theirs. We can live with whatever discomfort we experience. Instead of avoiding the discomfort, lean into it. Remember, this discomfort is how we learn and do better. Please embrace it.

Sometimes the Loudest thing a white woman can do are the quietest of acts. Listening, learning, lifting, sharing, believing, and trusting are all ways to support women of color. As you do, use your voice to help make things better for them. Use your voice to educate other white women about racism. Use your voice to ensure we do not have any more twenty-six-year-old black women dying in their apartments because of botched drug raids.

It won't be perfect. You will make mistakes. Swallow your pride and keep going. As White Loud Women, our roles are critical in bring equality and justice to the lives of women of color. Racism will not be fixed by people of color. It can only be fixed by white people. Are you ready to step up to the plate and help?

66

RISING TIDE

I magine you are sitting near a shore. Around you, boats of different shapes and sizes are tied to docks. The waves rise and fall, lapping the shore, and the boats bob with each passing wave. It's low tide, and you can see the hermit crabs scurrying along the shore.

As you sit there, you notice a change in the water current. The tide is coming in. As it does, you notice something else: As the ocean waves fill the harbor, the boats rise. The big boats, the little boats, the red boats, and the white boats, too. They rise together as the tide swells under them.

That's because a rising tide lifts all boats.

I love this saying because it shows how we can do amazing things with a force under us, elevating our boats so we gain momentum and head mightily to our destination.

Those boats? They are Loud Women.

The rising tide? That's us banded together.

Remember my story about the child protection officer? She was part of my tide. The investigator joined forces with my son's pediatrician, psychiatrist, therapist, fellow supportive moms, and family to form a rising tide that not only calmed my rocking boat, but also helped me see the horizon. They banded together to show what I could not see from the stern of my boat: *Everything was going to be okay.*

And it was. While my captaining was part of this success, this rising tide of supportive women played an integral part.

I am proud of myself for accepting their help, too. Your boat cannot make the journey alone. You need your captaining prowess, for sure, but you also need the rising tide, the wind in your sails, and a compass to guide you. Boats do not decline the help from the tide or the winds. You shouldn't either.

Be your boat and accept help from the strong, rising tide of Loud Women.

Be a Loud Woman and become someone's rising tide, too.

These boats, these tides—it's how we get through this journey together. Let's grip our captain's steering wheels, put up our sails, check our compasses, and go. Remember to trust the tide under you. Fellow Loud Women are there, supporting and lifting you through calm and rocky seas. You got this because we have you.

A rising tide lifts all boats. A Loud Woman tide lifts all Loud Women.

67

DIFFERENCES

L oud Women will get Louder in different ways—and that's okay. It is intended to be a different journey for each of us. No matter her journey, it's important that we support her.

You may have a difficult time, though, supporting a Loud Woman when she has different ideologies, philosophies, or lifestyles than you. I know I have difficulties supporting women who backed Donald Trump.

Take, for example, Kellyanne Conway. Did you know that Kellyanne is the first woman to have run a successful U.S. presidential campaign? She is a genius pollster, having owned her own polling firm and worked on campaigns for former Speaker of the House Newt Gingrich and Senator Ted Cruz (among others). [43]

As a feminist, I applaud Kellyanne's accomplishments. She has excelled in a male-dominated field and accomplished a major "first" for women in the U.S.

As a feminist, she also drives me crazy because I do not share her views on abortion and her support of President Trump. My head is full of "buts" when I think of Kellyanne. She's a brilliant pollster *but* used her skills to help Trump get elected. She's a feminist *but* does not trust women to make their own reproductive decisions. She's an intelligent woman, *but* she makes up crap during news interviews. She's a mom *but* has made many public mistakes about her daughter, Claudia. But, but, BUT!

How do I reconcile this? How do I support a woman like Kellyanne when I disagree with so much of what she believes and says?

Here's how: Think of support as divided into two buckets.

The first bucket is to support the freedom to choose how you want to be Loud. You do not have to agree with the Loud Woman's choices, but you can support how *she's free to make her own choices*. Isn't that what feminism is all about—the freedom to choose? The choice to be a stay-at-home mom or work-away-from-home mom? To apply to law school or not? To wear a dress or not? To have an abortion or not? To support a particular president or not?

Feminism wants these choices available to all women without restriction, bias, or discrimination. In the case of Kellyanne Conway, she chose to use her brilliance to help Donald Trump get elected. That is her choice—one she is free to make. At the end of the day, she must rest her head on her pillow and be content with her choices.

So, I can support Kellyanne's freedom to make the choice that feels right to her—even if I do not agree with the choice she made. That's how I support a Loud Woman who is opposite from me in key ideological areas. I support the existence of choices, and the ability a Loud Woman to choose the path she wants to follow. I may hate the path she has chosen, but I will always support that choices are available to her.

The second bucket is to support what a Loud Woman chooses. This is more whole-hearted support. In terms of politics, I can whole-heartedly support women such as Vice President Kamala Harris, Senator Elizabeth Warren, or Representative Katie Porter. They believe in the same things I do—and fight for them. They make the same ideological and philosophical choices as me. This takes support to the fullest level, right? Not only do I support that these Loud Women *have* choices (Bucket #1), I also support the choices they have made because it aligns with my thinking (Bucket #2). Is this shallow? No. It's just an extra level of support. It would be shallow to not support women's choices, but it is *not* shallow to disagree with their choices.

Yes, you will have an easier time supporting women who share the same philosophies as you. This does not always mean politics. You may have a certain philosophy about how to raise children, or a certain philosophy on how to invest your money. We like to support people who are like us—and that's true for Loud Women's Journeys, too. This is being human, and if you found a Loud Woman who you can whole-heartedly support, then pour from Bucket #2 all day long.

During the early stages of the confirmation of Supreme Court Justice Amy Coney Barrett, someone tweeted that feminists are hypocrites for not supporting the nominee because she adopted and raised seven children while being a successful judge. This is someone who wants *all* feminists to pour from *both* buckets. But you do not have to. You can support her from Bucket #1 and acknowledge her judicial accomplishments, applaud her for adopting kids, and congratulate her on being appointed to the Supreme Court. That's being a supportive feminist. But you do not have to support her views (Bucket #2). This does not make you any less of a feminist. It makes you a human being with different viewpoints. And you are allowed to not support her appointment to the Supreme Court, for example, because of her viewpoints. You are still a feminist. You are still supporting Loud Women. Don't let those who try to manipulate what feminism is convince you otherwise.

Now, let's talk about women who choose to be racist, sexist, homophobic, or adopt any other form of prejudice out there. It's different to have an ideological difference, such as how much money the government should spend on bombs or roads. It's quite another to have a prejudiced view on race, sex, and gay people. While feminism advocates for your right to choose, this does not mean you get to be a shitty human being. Racism, sexism, homophobia, and xenophobia are not political ideologies; they are prejudices. And if you choose to embrace a prejudice, *there is no bucket for you.*

I am probably a starry-eyed Pollyanna, but I believe we are more alike than different. I think we all want women to get Louder. It's my hope that women who are clinging to their prejudices may change their minds if other Loud Women help them. Prejudice stems from fear, and often you are afraid of what you do not know or understand. To reach this level of knowing, it takes other Loud Women to educate you. Some are lost causes. However, many have not been exposed to the effects of their prejudice on other people's lives, and with this exposure and heartfelt conversations, prejudices can go away. I believe this with all my heart.

If I could sit down with a white woman who responds "All Lives Matter!" when she sees Black Lives Matter, I would tell her that she is correct. Of course, all lives matter. And then I would explain that for black people in the U.S., they are subjected to prejudice by our justice and legal system—something she cannot understand as a white woman. In many cases, the actions of police officers do not show that they value black lives. In many other cases, the legal system does not show that they support black lives either. And only when white people say *and believe* that "Black Lives Matter" will this change. Maybe if this woman hears this from enough people, her mind will change, too.

The great thing about having a choice means you can learn from them and make better decisions in the future. I am sure we have all chosen to do something that we later regretted, and we would make different decisions if we could do it over again. We may not get a chance for a do over, but we can learn from those choices. And we can learn from the choices—both good and bad—made by other Loud Women. And what better way to learn about other Loud Women's choices, consequences, regrets, and lessons than by having whole-hearted conversations? Sometimes the gift of conversation can be the best support we can give a Loud Woman who is so different from us on many things. Openness and understanding are priceless. Again, I may be a starry-eyed Pollyanna, but I think it's worth a shot.

How else will this world change?

BELIEVE

Why is our first instinct, as women, *not* to believe women, especially when it comes to sexism and men abusing her in some way?

When a woman says something is sexist, *believe her*.
When a woman accuses a man of rape, *believe her*.
When a woman accuses someone of sexual harassment, *believe her*.
When a woman says her husband is beating her, *believe her*.

We should because statistically, women are telling the truth. Just look at these sexual violence statistics gathered by the National Sexual Violence Resource Center (NSVRC) and the Human Rights Campaign:

- 18.3% of all U.S women have been raped.[44]
- Nine out of ten rape victims are women.[45]
- In 2018, the self-reported incidence of rape doubled from the previous year. However, in 2018, the number of reported rapes dropped—from 40% in 2017 to 25% in 2018.[46]

- A 2016 study of urban black women reported that 53.7% of them were raped.[47]
- For Native Americans and Alaska Natives, 56.1% of women reported sexual violence.[48]
- 46% of bisexual women have been raped (compared to 13% of lesbians and 17% of straight women).[49]
- According to the 2015 U.S. Transgender Survey, 47% of transgender people have been sexually assaulted.[50]
- 85% of victim advocates report that an LGBTQ rape victims were denied services because of their sexual orientation or gender identity.[51]

Furthermore, sexual assault victims do not report their crimes to the police. According to RAINN (Rape, Abuse, & Incest National Network), "only 230 out of every 1,000 sexual assaults are reported to the police. That means about three out of four go unreported."[52]

Let's see what happens when women do report these crimes:

- Sixty women accused Bill Cosby of rape, drugging, sexual assault, and coercion, but many people still think he is innocent and that these women are after his money.
- Twenty-six women have accused Donald Trump of sexual misconduct, and his supporters say it is just a way to blemish his reputation as president.
- Three women accused Supreme Court Justice Brett Kavanaugh of sexual misconduct, including attempted rape, but it was written off as a Democratic conspiracy to prevent the judge from becoming a Supreme Court justice.

And when I say "many people" or "supporters" in these sentences, these are groups of men *and women*.

Just like we have been taught to not trust ourselves, we have also been taught not to trust each other. Societal conditioning says women are untrustworthy. As a result, when a woman accuses someone, especially a man, of a wrongdoing, our first instinct is to not believe her.

Our entire justice system is built on this premise. Look at what happens during rape and sexual assault cases that are brought to trial. The woman's entire body must first be examined for the rape kit. She will endure questions about her sexual past (to make her look like a slut), her drinking and drug habits (to make her look like a bad decision-maker), and what she was wearing (to make it look like she was asking for it).

If you want a firsthand account of the injustices rape and sexual assault victims endure, read *Know My Name* by Chanel Miller.

Brock Taylor sexually assaulted Chanel behind a dumpster at Stanford University. She passed out from alcohol consumption, and Brock took advantage by sexually assaulting Chanel, including putting his fingers in her vagina. He was caught, red-handed, by two Swedish exchange students. Yet, he still proclaimed she consented. So, they went to trial, and what Chanel had to endure from the court system was appalling.

Equally appalling were the comments Chanel read online about herself. She was called a slut and whore, and told she got what was coming to her. And not just by men. Women typed these messages too.

The angry part of me believes there's a cold place in hell for women who do not believe another woman when she has been treated badly by a man.

Why does this anger me so?

Because a woman has endured something horrible—abuse from her partner, a sexist comment, an unwanted sexual advance—and we automatically dismiss her. She is a *victim,* but we tend to believe the accuser (who in most cases are men).

I want to challenge us to believe Loud Women. In most cases, she is telling the truth. Time and time again, we see that to be the case, but we get amnesia and fall back to our default position of *do not believe her.*

When Christine Blasey Ford testified to Congress about Justice Kavanaugh's attempted rape, I saw firsthand how women do not believe other women. I made a promise to myself that I would not be one of these women. I would rather be wrong about a woman's accusation than to not believe her. I would rather be eating humble pie than not support a woman who has made a serious accusation.

I beg you, Loud Woman, do the same. Our sisters need us to believe them. It is hard enough to endure the pain they have experienced without the support of fellow women. It's the least we can do, especially considering the hard road ahead as she fights for justice, much less an apology. That hard road will be so much more tolerable if we bear witness and believe her.

69

STUPID

The day after the vice-presidential debate between Mike Pence and Kamala Harris, I saw a post from a conservative female friend that read, "Is she really this stupid?"

I did not need to be a soothsayer to know who this friend was referring to: Kamala Harris.

Like driving past a car wreck, I proceeded to the comments, and my jaw dropped:

- Many said "yes," agreeing that Senator Harris was "really this stupid."
- Several commented that they hated her "smirk."
- Two women wanted to slap Senator Harris.
- Several referred to her as a *biatch* (intentionally misspelled so it did not set off the Facebook censors)
- Another said she was master of "talking down to someone."
- Another said "her facial expressions are killing me."
- A woman remarked she "can't stomach listening to her."
- Someone posted a GIF implying Harris was "the devil incarnate."

- And finally, a guy commented that the stupid ones are those who vote for Biden and Harris.

(The disparaging comments continued, but I could not read another word.)

Let's first address the sexist double standard here. Every person who commented is a Trump supporter. President Trump is known for smirks, talking down to people, and a plethora of facial expressions.

Did these people have the same reaction to him? No, and not just because he's a Republican. It's because he's a white guy, and Kamala Harris is a woman of color. Make no mistake. Female politicians, especially ones of color, are held to a higher standard than their male counterparts. This social media conversation proves it.

Equally appalling was the fact that people think Senator Harris is stupid.

Let's be clear: Senator Harris is not stupid. She is a smart, compassionate, educated woman. You can call her a lot of things, but stupid is not one of them.

A woman is not stupid because she disagrees with your politics. You can disagree with her stance, think she is wrong about her beliefs, and roll your eyes at her plans, but it is not acceptable to call another woman stupid. Ever.

This happens to women, no matter what their political ideology is. I have seen similar disparaging comments about conservative women, such as Kellyanne Conway, Sarah Huckabee Sanders, and Sarah Palin. These women are not stupid either.

Stupid is one of the meanest, most condescending things you can say about a Loud Woman. We may not win any battles against men with our bodily strength, but we can win with our mind. When another woman calls a Loud Woman "stupid," it is akin to saying her brain and intelligence are not worthy, and she has no business opening her mouth. It is a way to shut up and shut down a Loud Woman, and it can feel like a sucker punch to the gut.

Of course, stupid is just one word in our repertoire. Idiot, bitch, slut, whore, cunt, dumb, and many more creep into our vocabulary. If you can stomach it, look at the comments women make to each other on a news article. It's not just keyboard confidence at play; it is long-held societal conditioning that tells us it is okay to use derogatory names against other women.

Our patriarchal society is at fault for pitting us against each other. Just look at the movies where two women fight over the affection of a man. In *Fatal Attraction*, Glenn Close's character boiled the family's pet rabbit to get the attention of her married lover. Even comedies such as *Monster-in-Law* pit two women, Jane Fonda and Jennifer Lopez, against each other, competing over the affection of the son and fiancé.

Then, we have the movies where women are competing against each other for jobs and promotions. *The Devil Wears Prada* pits Emily Blunt and Anne Hathaway against each other while Meryl Streep's character shows the stereotypical portrayal of a woman in charge (cold, mean, and heartless). *Black Swan* makes every ballerina look like a competitive, cruel bitch who writes "whore" on mirrors and accuses the other of sleeping her way to the top.

Even in high school or your local bar, a crowd loves a good "cat fight," and people practically climb on top of each other to watch two women fight. Why do you think mud wrestling is a thing?

Yes, women fighting and calling each other names are exactly what the patriarchal society wants, but that does not mean we have to oblige.

Loud Women, check the language we use to describe other women, even if she has a different political stance than you. Calling another woman "stupid" is not helping *any* woman. It falls right into the trap set up by our patriarchal society.

This will be hard because our societal conditioning will need to be unraveled and woven back together. But we can do it, Loud Women. We can.

Let's stop calling each other stupid. It's the right first step. Are you with me?

70

BULLYING

One time, a blogger wrote about how she was disappointed in herself for not supporting a female entrepreneur who was getting bullied constantly on Instagram. This entrepreneur posted about positive body image and shared pictures of her body, which prompted comments about her being "fat." The blogger read these hateful comments but never spoke up to defend this woman. Eventually, the bullying and criticism got to this Loud Woman, and she closed her business.

We cannot have Loud Women bullied to the point where they are closing their businesses. That is not how we change the world!

With stories like this, it's no wonder Loud Women resist using social media to express their Loudness. Hateful comments, Internet trolls, and cyberbullies are rampant. Keyboard confidence buttresses these spiteful people, and if you have ever been on the receiving end of their nastiness, you know how it can make you feel: outraged, scared, anxious, even depressed.

Some folks will say "just get a thicker skin," but it should not matter. It is deplorable how these jerks come after you for expressing your opinion (often on your *own* social media profile). It sucks we have to deal with them, but here we are.

Online bullies may never go away, which is why we need to strengthen our resolve. How do we do this? By remembering this truth: *Someone's opinion of you is none of your business.* It is a hard truth to accept, thanks to years of believing otherwise, but if you can accept it, you will strengthen your resolve.

You can also strengthen your resolve by remembering that feedback and criticism are someone else's feedback—*not facts.* Their comments, especially the negative ones, are a mirror reflecting what is going on with them—not you. Again, this takes practice, but if you can embrace this truth, your resolve will be rock solid.

While you are working on your own resolve, you also can help other Loud Women work on theirs. When a Loud Woman makes a brave post on social media, and someone is a jerk about it, be a good community member and step in. Help a Loud Woman out when someone is calling her terrible names, like this:

Loud Woman: I believe a woman has a right to make her own healthcare decisions about her body, including when she is pregnant.

Asshole: It's not your body anymore when you are pregnant! You should have thought about this because you slept with some guy. Just keep your legs closed, you cunt, and then you won't have to kill a baby.

(Note: This is a made-up conversation, but if you look at any anti-abortion article, you will find this sort of "discourse.")

Now, if you see a conversation like this on social media, what do you usually do? Probably keep scrolling, right?

Here is the problem with scrolling by: You just left this Loud Woman out to dry. Now I am sure she is a grown-ass woman and can take care of herself, but wouldn't it be nice if she felt supported? It would, and that's where Loud Women like you and me step in.

First, I would report this asshole's comment because he called her a cunt. That's a defamatory word and should not be tolerated on social media platforms. Whether the site decides to do something about it is out of your hands, but you should report it anyway.

Second, show your support to the Loud Woman by replying to her post or comment. Do so imperfectly by agreeing with her or cheering her on. Often, Loud Women get caught up in making the perfect statement, and when it does not happen, she abandons her response. Imperfect responses are better than no responses. A simple *thank you for posting this* or *I agree with you so much* can work wonders for a Loud Woman who is sticking her neck out there.

You may be tempted to respond directly to the asshole, but please remember two things. You are feeding the troll, which often sets off further spite and gives the asshole great pleasure. Second, you can get yourself banned from social media sites (I know this one from experience).

One time, in a community Facebook Group, a female nurse thanked a local restaurant for providing a free dinner to her Emergency Room department. The coronavirus pandemic was just beginning, and she felt gratitude for the community support. However, one asshole commented that this nurse was unprofessional because her personal profile included the #StayTheFuckHome message. Now, this message was not evident on this nurse's post. He had to click through and find it.

Here's a nurse who risked her life to take care of people sick with COVID, and this asshole responds by calling her unprofessional for *fuck* on her personal profile.

My sense of outrage grew, and I refused to let this nurse get belittled. I told that asshole that the nurse is a grown woman who can have whatever she wants on her profile, including fuck, and to take his cuss word policing somewhere else.

Well, guess who got muted from this group for five days because of this conversation? ME! Why? Because I said *fuck* in my response. It did not matter that this asshole berated a female nurse, calling her unprofessional after he dug around her personal Facebook profile. As soon as I said *fuck*, I could not post in the Facebook group for five days. Additionally, my comment was deleted, so I have no idea if the nurse read my comment. I hope she did.

That's why I recommend ignoring the assholes. Instead, respond directly to the Loud Woman. To me, it is most important for the Loud Woman to know I am in her corner.

Trolls and assholes may always be a part of our social media experiences, but a Loud Woman should not have to battle them alone. When you support a Loud Woman on social media, she not only feels supported, she also knows that you witnessed the abuse. When you get attacked online, it is horrible to feel like you are alone. When you support her, it strengthens her resolve so she can continue being Loud —not just on social media but in all aspects of her life.

Is this scary? You bet. I was scared shitless when I first started defending Loud Women (and getting muted for five days did not help), but the more I do it, the more confident I get.

Please do not let fear stop you from helping out a fellow Loud Woman who is getting bullied online. She may be fearful too, but she mustered up enough courage to express her opinion and champion for something she believed in, knowing she may be attacked. That's brave, in my opinion. You can match her bravery but ensuring she is not standing there alone. Speak up. Have some keyboard confidence too, but use it to lift someone who could use your love and support. We cannot let Loud Women feel so picked on that they stop what they're doing. That would be the biggest travesty of all. We *can* prevent it, together, by never letting a fellow Loud Woman stand alone on social media.

71

FAITH KEEPERS

My Faith Keepers are a group of bad-ass women who elevate my soul. Together, we are six women entrepreneurs. Separately, we have unique Gifts that are changing the world. Nicole channels from Source, teaches about tapping into your intuition, and is my spiritual mentor. Carrie teaches creative entrepreneurs how to move their bodies to unblock their minds. JKC is a profit engineer, helping entrepreneurs make money so they can live the life of their dreams. Clare is a business coach who helps entrepreneurs get out of their way so they can grow their businesses in a way that supports their lifestyle —without burning them out in the process. And Debby is a publisher, bringing books into the world so these stories heal and transform others.

We are different ages with different accents and energy levels, but we share a common goal: illuminating each other's potential. Showing what her potential is, for sure, but also how to tap into it and live a Louder life.

I picked up the term "Faith Keepers" from Maria Shriver's book, *I've Been Thinking*. She writes, "One of my girlfriends refers to her other girlfriends as 'faith keepers.' It's such a beautiful way to put it, and it's true. My girlfriends keep the faith for me when I can't find it within myself. And I do it for them. And that's what we all need to do." [53]

The Faith Keepers not only keep us in faith, they also hold up a mirror to each of us, and that mirror reflects back the version they see —the ultimate personification of our potential.

My Faith Keepers all believe when we lean into our potential and do bigger things, not only will our lives change for the better, our world will, too. Each of us has a God-given gift, and we know it is important for us to embrace this Gift and be Loud about it.

If one of us tries to shrink away from her potential, we show her the vision we see, and remind her of her great potential and Gifts. We nudge her out of hiding, showering her with positive messages and reminders that the world needs her Gifts to heal and grow.

Our monthly Zoom calls are filled with laughter and tears, pep talks and truth bombs, ideas and constructive criticism. We check our Egos at the door and listen with our whole hearts. Our advice is shrouded in love but never untruths. We do not say things for the sake of saying them; instead we advise and question because we know the stakes are high. Each of us has such immense brilliance, and collectively, we are a tsunami-level force that can do anything. We have written books, changed business directions, buried our parents, survived a global pandemic, and bemoaned the antics of our children.

We have purchased from each other, been the lone audience member on Facebook Lives, and provided blurbs to help market our books.

We do not do these things out of forced obligation. We do it because we are connected through our purpose and potential, and when one of us rises, the others do too.

This book, for example, is a product of my Faith Keepers' support. Over and over again, my Faith Keepers held up a mirror to show me what they see: a mentor, author, and speaker who inspires women to lead more fulfilling lives. A Loud Woman who understands the challenges we face and how to overcome them. A mentor who will not rest until every woman in her circle gets bolder, more confident, and less selfless. A woman who believes that to see the change in the world, we must elevate *all* women—for its the women who will shepherd in the changes this world so desperately needs.

When they first showed this to me, I did not believe it. My Faith Keepers are a stubborn bunch, though, and when they see a vision, they continue to hold up that mirror until I see it too. Their reminders have brought me to where I am today, and this book you are holding is the result of my Faith Keepers' love and support.

One of my greatest joys in mentoring female entrepreneurs is to hold a mirror in front of them to show them what I see. Like me, they often resist at first, but with time and my loving nudges, they begin to see it too. My nudges become their Truth, and their image starts to match the image I am reflecting back to them.

And when it clicks, my goodness, it is a beautiful sight to see. Her eyes brim with tears and she smiles uncontrollably, and she says, sometimes in a whisper, sometimes as an exclamation, "Yes! This is what I am meant to do!" And then she does it.

Often, we cannot see the whole picture of our potential because our Ego and subconscious thoughts cloud our lens. That's where other Loud Women, your Faith Keepers, come in. Your Faith Keepers can see it. They can hold that Faith for you, being the keeper of this flame until you are ready to take it over.

After you see this vision of your potential, they stay by your side because they know you will need them along the way. Plus, they are invested in your success at a soul level; they could not leave you if they tried. They also know your flame might flicker and threaten to burn out—and that sometimes the weight of your flame can become heavy. That's when your Faith Keepers step in and help lighten the load. They will not let you stop, but they will show you how to rest and replenish. Your Faith Keepers will strengthen your spirit with their love and support, and you will continue on your journey, blanketed in the faith of these Loud Women.

Loud Women, who are your Faith Keepers? If you do not have any, look around because I bet they are out there, just waiting for you to say "I need you." Look for the ones with those mirrors and crazy-sounding ideas. Those are your Faith Keepers. Those are the Loud Women who see your great potential—and help you see it, too.

Don't forget: You are someone's Faith Keeper, too. It's a role to cherish. Thank you for helping other Loud Women tap into their Gifts and live their lives to its fullest expression. It's an important, sacred job—one that will reward you in many ways.

Stay in faith, Loud Woman. I see you. I honor you. I support you. The paths on our journey may be treacherous at times but do not despair. Allow your Faith Keepers to remind you of your potential. Allow your Faith Keepers to lift you. Allow your Faith Keepers to lighten the load when you need it. Their collective faith will always light the way for you. All you have to do is lift your head and look for their light.

EPILOGUE

When I am brave enough to say goodbye
I'll use the wings you gave me
and away I'll fly.

— CELIA MCMAHON

72

GOOD-BYE

L oud Woman, I struggled with creating a subtitle for this book. My editor and I exchanged several rounds of wordplay before *Good-bye, Inner Good Girl!* emerged like a welcome wave from a friend.

Good-bye, Inner Good Girl.

Our Inner Good Girl is what we know, what we've been taught, and where we feel the most secure. For sure, our Inner Good Girl made everyone else comfortable. It may be hard to bid her good-bye.

But we must say good-bye to her because it's time for your transformation into a Loud Woman.

Just like we said good-bye to our childhood dolls and middle school lip gloss, it's time to say good-bye to our Inner Good Girl—to allow her to be part of our memories, for better or worse. I don't know about yours, but my Inner Good Girl is fucking exhausted, and she's ready for retirement.

It's hard work being a Good Girl, after all.

It's hard to squelch your true self, to live a life where you avoid fears, bite your tongue, let people tell you what to do. It's hard being polite all the time. It's hard to constantly ignore your intuition.

You don't have to do it anymore.

Because you're a Loud Woman now. You now know what to do to

get Louder. Will this work be hard, too? Absolutely. But the difference between Good Girl work and Loud Woman work is this: Your Loud Woman work feels better. It feels right. It doesn't feel like you're going against your inner grain anymore. And that's why, even though it's hard work, it's gratifying work—and you'll keep going, imperfectly.

Take one baby step after another. You've taken baby steps before, you know. And you fell and cried and let others help you get up—but you didn't stop. You tried again. And again. And those baby steps became confident steps until you ran forth in this world, in total glee and without a care.

Run in glee,

Loud Woman.

For you are free.

You are free.

You are free.

LOUD WOMAN CREDO

We, as Loud Women, believe we are worthy of everything we desire.

We, as Loud Women, are feminists who believe women should have equality and the freedom to choose what's best for our lives.

We, as Loud Women, create boundaries to protect our bodies, minds, souls, energies, and whatever else is important to us.

We, as Loud Women, shed traditional, patriarchal manners that do not serve us.

We, as Loud Women, know fear will always be there, but we don't let fear stop us from getting Louder in our lives.

We, as Loud Women, shatter comfort zones.

We, as Loud Women, trust ourselves, knowing we are the best expert in what's best for our lives.

We, as Loud Women, support other Loud Women.

We, as Loud Women, say good-bye to our Inner Good Girl, tucking her in with love and grace.

ENDNOTES

WORTHY

ASK AND PERSIST

[1] Morin, Amy. Essay. In *13 Things Mentally Strong Women Don't Do: Own Your Power, Channel Your Confidence, and Find Your Authentic Voice for a Life of Meaning and Joy*, 127–27. New York, NY: William Morrow, an imprint of HarperCollins Publishers, 2020.

[2] Caldwell, Leigh Ann, Frank Thorp V, and Andrew Rafferty. "Warren Silenced for Reading Coretta Scott King Letter at Sessions Debate." NBCNews.com. NBCUniversal News Group, February 9, 2017. https://www.nbcnews.com/politics/congress/sen-elizabeth-warren-barred-speaking-impugning-sen-jeff-sessions-n718166.

COMPENSATION

[3] Sonam, Sheth, Madison Hoff. "These 8 Charts Show the Glaring Gap between Men's and Women's Salaries in the US." Business Insider.

Business Insider, March 24, 2021. https://www.businessinsider.com/gender-wage-pay-gap-charts-2017-3.

[4] Ibid.

[5] Ibid.

[6] Ibid.

[7] McCarriston, Shanna. "USWNT Equal Pay Lawsuit: Everything You Need to Know about the Women's World Cup Champions' Legal Fight." CBSSports.com, July 11, 2019. https://www.cbssports.com/soccer/news/uswnt-equal-pay-lawsuit-everything-you-need-to-know-about-the-womens-world-cup-champions-legal-fight/.

[8] Fletcher, Jessica, and Stephanie Yang. "The USWNT Lawsuit Timeline." Stars and Stripes FC. Stars and Stripes FC, February 3, 2017. https://www.starsandstripesfc.com/2017/2/3/14498152/complete-updated-uswnt-ussf-cba-negotiation-timeline.

[9] McCarriston, Shanna. "USWNT Equal Pay Lawsuit: Everything You Need to Know about the Women's World Cup Champions' Legal Fight." CBSSports.com, July 11, 2019. https://www.cbssports.com/soccer/news/uswnt-equal-pay-lawsuit-everything-you-need-to-know-about-the-womens-world-cup-champions-legal-fight/.

[10] Ibid.

[11] Booker, Brakkton. "U.S. Soccer Apologizes For Saying Male Players Have 'More Responsibility' Than Women." NPR. NPR, March 11, 2020. https://www.npr.org/2020/03/11/814656567/male-players-have-more-responsibility-than-women-u-s-soccer-says-in-court-filing.

[12] Cater, Franklyn. "Federal Judge Dismisses U.S. Women's Soccer Team's Equal Pay Claim." NPR. NPR, May 2, 2020. https://www.n-

pr.org/2020/05/02/849492863/federal-judge-dismisses-u-s-womens-
soccer-team-s-equal-pay-claim#:~:text=The%20U.S.%20women%20-
filed%20the,money%20than%20their%20male%20counterparts.

[13] Ibid.

[14] Codinha, Cotton. "Hearts in the Game." *Allure Magazine*, August
2020.

FEMINISM

REGRET

[15] Timm, Jane C. "Trump on Hot Mic: 'When You're a Star ... You Can
Do Anything' to Women." NBCNews.com. NBCUniversal News
Group, February 7, 2017. https://www.nbcnews.com/politics/2016-
election/trump-hot-mic-when-you-re-star-you-can-do-n662116.

[16] Dr. Jenna Eilis, opinion contributor. "'Women's March' Feminists
Want Entitlements, Not Equality." The Hill, March 8, 2017.
https://thehill.com/blogs/pundits-blog/civil-rights/322964-womens-
march-feminists-dont-want-equality-they-want.

[17] Venker, Suzanne. "Feminists Want Women to Be Liberated from
Men, Marriage and Children -- No Wonder They Never Use the
Word." Fox News. FOX News Network, December 15, 2017.
https://www.foxnews.com/opinion/feminists-want-women-to-be-
liberated-from-men-marriage-and-children-no-wonder-they-never-use-
the-word.

[18] Staff, Written by Media Matters. "Limbaugh: 'Feminism Was Estab-
lished So As To Allow Unattractive Women Easier Access To The
Mainstream Of Pop Culture.'" Media Matters for America. Accessed
April 5, 2021. https://www.mediamatters.org/rush-limbaugh/lim-

baugh-feminism-was-established-so-allow-unattractive-women-easier-access.

[19] Adichie, Chiamanda Ngozi. In *We Should All Be Feminists*, 48. New York, NY: Anchor, 2014.

[20] Ajayi, Luvvie. *I'm Judging You: The Do-Better Manual*, 118-119. New York, NY: Henry Holt and Company, 2017.

[21] Dastagir, Alia E. "A Feminist Glossary Because We Didn't All Major in Gender Studies." USA Today. Gannett Satellite Information Network, March 21, 2018. https://www.usatoday.com/story/news/2017/03/16/feminism-glossary-lexicon-language/99120600/.

[22] Person. "Word to Live By: Gloria Steinem." CR Fashion Book. CR Fashion Book, August 20, 2019. https://www.crfashionbook.com/celebrity/g28709044/gloria-steinem-quotes/?slide=1.

INTERSECTIONAL FEMINISM

[23] "Intersectional Feminism: What It Means and Why It Matters Right Now." UN Women, July 20, 2020. https://www.un-women.org/en/news/stories/2020/6/explainer-intersectional-feminism-what-it-means-and-why-it-matters.

BOUNDARIES

NOTIFICATIONS

[24] Saad, Syeda Khaula. "What Happens To Your Brain When You Get A Phone Notification." Bustle. Bustle, November 15, 2019. https://www.bustle.com/p/what-happens-to-your-brain-when-you-get-a-phone-notification-19256076.

TIM AND DENISE

25 "Contact." The Blog of Author Tim Ferriss, January 21, 2020. https://tim.blog/contact/.

26 "Contact: Denise Duffield Thomas: Money Mindset Mentor for Women." Contact | Denise Duffield Thomas | Money Mindset Mentor for Women. Accessed April 6, 2021. https://www.denisedt.com/contact.

MANNERS

MANSPREADER

27 "Manspreading." Wikipedia. Wikimedia Foundation, March 11, 2021. https://en.wikipedia.org/wiki/Manspreading.

EMOTIONAL

28 Adichie, Chiamanda Ngozi. In *We Should All Be Feminists*, 21-22. New York, NY: Anchor, 2014.

29 Moore, Steve. "Steve Moore: What I Learned at the Women's March." Fox News. FOX News Network, January 24, 2017. https://www.foxnews.com/opinion/steve-moore-what-i-learned-at-the-womens-march.

30 Cillizza, Analysis by Chris. "We Should All Be Appalled by Donald Trump's Tweet about Greta Thunberg - CNN Politics." CNN. Cable News Network, December 13, 2019. https://www.cnn.-com/2019/12/12/politics/greta-thunberg-donald-trump/index.html.

FEAR

REJECTION

[31] Mohr, Tara. *Playing Big: Find Your Voice, Your Mission, Your Message*, 90-91. New York, NY: Avery, an imprint of Penguin Random House, 2015.

RISKY

[32] Ferriss, Timothy. *The 4-Hour Workweek: Escape 9-5, Live Anywhere, and Join the New Rich* 42. New York, NY: Crown publisher, 2007.

DISCOMFORT

COMFORT ZONES

[33] Morin, Amy. *13 Things Mentally Strong Women Don't Do: Own Your Power, Channel Your Confidence, and Find Your Authentic Voice for a Life of Meaning and Joy*, 128. New York, NY: William Morrow, an imprint of HarperCollins Publishers, 2020.

[34] Ibid., page 131.

IMPERFECT ACTION

[35] Dogs of War. "Full List of TV Shows with Fat Husbands and Skinny Wives." Crasstalk, January 19, 2013. https://crasstalk.-com/2013/01/full-list-of-tv-shows-with-fat-husbands-and-skinny-wives/.

SOCIAL GOOD

[36] Doyle, Glennon. *Untamed*, 268. New York, NY: Dial Press, 2020.

[37] Saad, Layla F. "I Need to Talk to Spiritual White Women about White Supremacy (Part One)." LAYLA F. SAAD, April 10, 2019. http://laylafsaad.com/poetry-prose/white-women-white-supremacy-1.

[38] Ajayi, Luvvie. *I'm Judging You: The Do-Better Manual*, 231. New York, NY: Henry Holt and Company, 2017.

TRUST

INTUITION

[39] Brown, Brené. "The Most Dangerous Stories We Make Up." Brené Brown, July 27, 2015. https://brenebrown.com/blog/2015/07/27/the-most-dangerous-stories-we-make-up.

SUPPORT

SOMETHING ABOUT HER

[40] Doyle, Glennon. *Untamed*, 285. New York, NY: Dial Press, 2020.

[41] Ibid.

WHITE WOMEN

[42] "Luvvie Ajayi Jones's (@Luvvie) Instagram Profile." Accessed April 6, 2021. https://www.instagram.com/luvvie/, Thursday, September 24, 2020.

DIFFERENCES

[43] "Kellyanne Conway." Wikipedia. Wikimedia Foundation, March 6, 2021. https://en.wikipedia.org/wiki/Kellyanne_Conway.

BELIEVE

[44] "Statistics." National Sexual Violence Resource Center. Accessed April 6, 2021. https://www.nsvrc.org/statistics.

[45] "Scope of the Problem: Statistics." RAINN. Accessed April 6, 2021. https://www.rainn.org/statistics/scope-problem.

[46] "Statistics." National Sexual Violence Resource Center. Accessed April 6, 2021. https://www.nsvrc.org/statistics.

[47] Ibid.

[48] Ibid.

[49] "Sexual Assault and the LGBTQ Community." HRC. Accessed April 6, 2021. https://www.hrc.org/resources/sexual-assault-and-the-lgbt-community.

[50] Ibid.

[51] Ibid.

[52] "The Criminal Justice System: Statistics." RAINN. Accessed April 6, 2021. https://www.rainn.org/statistics/criminal-justice-system.

FAITH KEEPERS

[53] Shriver, Maria. *I've Been Thinking ...: Reflections, Prayers, and Meditations for a Meaningful Life*, 107. New York, NY: Diversified Publishing, 2018.

RECOMMENDED READING

I believe our Loud Woman journey is a continuous one where we seek out the wisdom, advice, and pep talks of other Loud Women on their journeys. Here are some books I would recommend adding to your Loud Woman library. I love each one, and I think you will too.

- *We Should All Be Feminists* by Chimamanda Ngozi Adichie
- *I'm Judging You: The Do-Better Manual* by Luvvie Ajayi
- *Rising Strong: How the Ability to Reset Transforms the Way We Love, Love, Parent, and Lead* by Brene' Brown
- *Against Our Will: Men, Women, and Rape* by Susan Brownmiller
- *Untamed* by Glennon Doyle
- *Get Rich, Lucky Bitch! Release Your Money Blocks and Live a First-Class Life* by Denise Duffield-Thomas
- *Fight Like A Girl* by Clementine Ford
- *Embrace Your Magnificence: Get Out of Your Own Way and Live a Richer, Fuller, More Abundant Life* by Fabienne Fredrickson
- *The Feminine Mystique* by Betty Friedan
- *Empowering Women: A Guide to Loving Yourself, Breaking Rules and Bringing Good into Your Life* by Louise Hay
- *Professional Troublemaker: The Fear-Fighter Manual* by Luvvie Ajayi Jones
- *Worthy: Boost Your Self-Worth to Grow Your New Worth* by Nancy Levin
- *Believe IT: How To Go from Underestimated to Unstoppable* by Jamie Kern Lima
- *Entitled: How Male Privilege Hurts Women* by Kate Manne
- *Know My Name: A Memoir* by Chanel Miller
- *Playing Big: Practical Wisdom for Women Who Want To Speak Up, Create, and Lead* by Tara Mohr
- *13 Things Mentally Strong Women Don't Do* by Amy Morin

- *Becoming* by Michelle Obama
- *So You Want To Talk About Race* by Ijeoma Oluo
- *The Power of Receiving: A Revolutionary Approach to Giving Yourself the Life You Want and Deserve* by Amanda Owen
- *One Life* by Megan Rapinoe
- *Me and White Supremacy: Combat Racism, Change the World, and Become a Good Ancestor* by Layla Saad
- *I've Been Thinking...Reflections, Prayers, and Meditations for a Meaningful Life* by Maria Shriver
- *The Truth Will Set You Free, But First It Will Piss You Off!: Thoughts on Life, Love, and Rebellion* by Gloria Steinem
- *Unbound: A Woman's Guide to Power* by Kasia Urbaniak
- *Forward: A Memoir* by Abby Wambach
- *Wolfpack: How To Come Together, Unleash Our Power, and Change the Game* by Abby Wambach
- *Mary Magdalene Revealed: The First Apostle, Her Feminist Gospel & the Christianity We Haven't Tried Yet* by Meggan Watterson
- *Educated: A Memoir* by Tara Westover

ACKNOWLEDGMENTS

I opened *Loud Woman* with a dedication to my mom, so it feels fitting to open up my acknowledgements with a thank you to Mom, too. Mom, you taught me from a young age to stick up for myself, believe in my abilities, and trust I could do anything I set my mind to. You embody Loudness, and you have always inspired me. Thank you, Mom. I love you.

Loud Woman would not be the book it is without my wonderful friend and editor, Debby Kevin. Debby, thank you for your constant encouragement, support, and shared vision. Not only are you the best cheerleader, your ability to coax from me the right words has made *Loud Woman* a book filled with stories that women can relate to. From the bottom of my heart, thank you for everything!

Thank you to my wonderful sister, Sandie, for rooting for me as I wrote this book. I appreciate your love and suggestions as you read my beta version. I am thrilled that your writing career is so successful and proud to follow in your footsteps. You're the best big sister a Loud Woman could ask for!

I am blessed to be surrounded with amazing networks of women who are my constant supporters. To my Faith Keepers, where would I be without you? I know: miserable in a cubicle somewhere. Thank you, ladies, for everything. To my Highlander Press cohort, thank you for accompanying me on this writing journey. What an awesome ride it has been! To my Celestial University students, Virtual Networkers, and book club members, you are the reason I do this. Thank you for being in my community!

Thank you to Rachel Taylor for taking my book cover vision and making it a reality. You have such an amazing knack for reading my mind. Special thank you to Pat Creedon for transforming Rachel's illustration into the final book cover.

I am so indebted to my beta readers for their help, guidance, advice, and general "you can do this" cheerleading. Patty Gaffney, Kai Gordon, Nicole Meltzer, Iman Salih, Amy Taliaferro, and Sandie Will, thank you for being such an integral part of this process.

Huge thank you to my dear friend, Shawna Jamiel, for constantly cheering me on and for partnering with me to establish Tampa Bay Basset Hounds. It's wonderful to have a friend who loves bassets as much as I do. I am also grateful to the Jamiel family for taking me under their wings like they've known me my entire life. And to all Tampa Bay Basset Hound families, thank you for attending the Meetups and sharing your wonderful dogs. It's truly the highlight of my day to see your beautiful bassets!

To the #bookstagrammers who enthusiastically agreed to read and review *Loud Woman*, thank you so much for everything you do for authors, especially your help in letting others know about *Loud Woman*.

To my launch partners, thank you for promoting *Loud Woman*. Words can't describe how much you rock!

Thank you to independent booksellers and local libraries for keeping the love of reading alive in our communities.

Thank you to healthcare workers, educators, and essential workers for all you do to make this world a better place.

And to you, dear reader, thank you for holding this book in your hands. I am honored that you have read *Loud Woman*.

Last, but never least, thank you to my supportive husband, Richard; my wonderful sons, Anthony and Joe; my bonus daughter, Faith; my basset girl, Trixie; and our always-amusing cats, Calamity Jane and Mr. Wu. I love my family. I am a blessed Loud Woman, for sure!

ABOUT JILL

Jill Celeste, MA, loves Loud Women and loud bassets. That's why you will likely find her teaching marketing and mindset to female entrepreneurs at Celestial University; or facilitating sisterhood and connection through her online networking organization, Virtual Networkers; or hanging out with basset hounds as the co-founder of Tampa Bay Basset Hounds. She lives near Tampa, Florida, with her husband, two sons, two cats, and a basset hound named Trixie. *Loud Woman* is her second book.

Photo by: Jaimi Weatherspoon

To learn more about Jill, please visit JillCeleste.com.

facebook.com/jillcelestepage
twitter.com/jill_celeste
instagram.com/jill_celeste

ABOUT HIGHLANDER PRESS

 Highlander Press, founded in 2019, is a mid-sized publishing company committed to diversity and sharing big ideas thereby changing the world through words. Highlander Press guides authors from where they are in the writing-editing-publishing process to where they have an impactful book of which they are proud, making a long-time dream come true. Having authored a book improves your confidence, helps create clarity, and ensures that you claim your expertise.

What makes Highlander Press unique is that our business model focuses on building strong collaborative relationships with other women-owned businesses, which specialize in some aspect of the publishing industry, such as graphic design, book marketing, book launching, copyrights, and publicity. The mantra "a rising tide lifts all boats" is one we embrace.

facebook.com/highlanderpress
instagram.com/highlanderpress
linkedin.com/in/highlanderpress

CPSIA information can be obtained
at www.ICGtesting.com
Printed in the USA
BVHW041312310821
615701BV00014B/379

9 781735 933337